W9-AZP-915

How Managers Make Things Happen

BY George S. Odiorne

PRENTICE-HALL, INC., Englewood Cliffs, N. J.

© 1961, BY

PRENTICE-HALL, INC.

ENGLEWOOD CLIFFS, N. J.

ALL RIGHTS RESERVED. NO PART OF THIS BOOK
MAY BE REPRODUCED IN ANY FORM, BY MIMEO-
GRAPH OR ANY OTHER MEANS, WITHOUT PER-
MISSION IN WRITING FROM THE PUBLISHER.

LIBRARY OF CONGRESS
CATALOG CARD NUMBER: 61-11217

Fifteenth Printing ..December, 1970

PRINTED IN THE UNITED STATES OF AMERICA

Preface

Since 1938 the author has spent nearly equal time between industrial employment in management positions and in the education of managers and would-be managers. Such august corporations as the American Can Company and General Mills Inc.; the American Management Association; and such excellent universities as Rutgers, New York University, and now Michigan have served the double purpose of providing him employment and a liberal business education concurrently. In addition to these permanent affiliations, the author has lectured, consulted, instructed and researched in management in several hundred other firms. This book is based on that combined study and experience.

In a corporate world become overwhelming with over-organization, red tape, complex controls, and powerful forces of inertia, it seems that there is a rising premium on the manager who can make things happen. The purpose of this book is to describe the various ways in which such action-getting managers think, behave, and relate to their environment so that they get results where others do not. If we learn from the experience of others, this book may be described as a "how to do it" book.

The presumption here is that many of the skills of getting things done have remained stable. The personal qualities of leadership and drive for goals is similar to those of classic leaders of past times. What is different however is the great change in the environment. The world in which today's manager must make things happen is wider in geographic scope, and his area of concern and responsibility is more complex than ever. The recognition of this expansion in scope is sometimes lacking. More often it's not recognized that being a manager in such an environment means that new and special forms of force and action are called for.

Social scientists, especially since the end of World War II have written and researched most extensively in the field of management action. Much of their writing and research has been carefully scrutinized, and is incorporated in this manual for management.

The author can't profess that these social scientists would agree at all with the use of some of their data, especially the general conclusion that action-centered management, as it is presently done, is essentially the manipulation of others. Yet, despite their protestations that manipulation is bad, they must face up to the plain facts that little other use has ever been made of their findings by the managers who read and apply their work.

Like business men who have gone to Washington with "businesslike ideas" only to discover to their dismay that they were babes in the woods in this foreign field, the social scientists of the past two decades have toddled into the field of business and been gobbled up by the managers there. Their insistence that the ethical strictures surrounding their findings be accepted along with their techniques have, of course, been adopted only to a minor degree by the profit and action-oriented managers. The work of the psychologist, sociologist, anthropologist, and economist have been used to market compact automobiles, to sell cosmetics and other equally useful products. More importantly it has been applied in the field of employee relations to alleviate the distress and discontent which free men feel in their work, and to provide palliatives in the relationships of the work place when one man has economic power over others.

This is hardly to suggest that the social scientists' influence hasn't been great nor their ethics wrong. The following pages are filled with applications which profit-minded professional managers can and do make of those findings. Social science as it wafts through the business organization has become a highly technical set of procedures for justifying the existing administrative arrangements, and arming certain individuals to manipulate rapidly through its heirarchies at the expense of others who chose to ignore these methods.

This book is addressed to managers who want to know how to make things happen. The basic presumption is that management today is aimed at profits and growth, and that the achievement of these goals requires mastery of new methods which the old-style manager did not require. Essentially this management job, as successful managers view it, is one of manipulating the environment, and most especially the people, in it. The objective of the book is to present some descriptive material on this manipulation.

Several of the chapters in this book have appeared as articles in *Nation's Business* and grateful acknowledgment is made to the publishers for permission to include them here. Further acknowledgment and gratitude are made to my wife Janet who suffered through its composition, assisted in editing copy, and typed the final manuscript.

Contents

Part I

GOOD MANAGERS MAKE THINGS HAPPEN

"Suddenly Hopkins whirled and faced him. *"Somebody has to do the big jobs!"* he said passionately. "This world was built by men like me! To really do a job you have to live it, body and soul! You people who just give half your mind to your work are riding on our backs."
"I know it," Tom said.

—SLOAN WILSON, *The Man in The Gray Flannel Suit*

Management Means Action—
Not Reaction

"People, it has been said, can be placed in three classes: the few who make things happen, the many who watch things happen, and the overwhelming majority who have no idea what has happened."

—NICHOLAS MURRAY BUTLER

In a metal working plant in the East two department managers were in competition for a plant manager's vacancy. The first was admittedly a good administrator. His knowledge of the affairs of his department was thorough and systematic. He worried over reports and controls which came to his desk daily, telling him how production, quality, safety, costs and spoilage were for the day or the week before. He established procedures and systems to feed back suggestions for improvement and better organization to the shop supervisors. He held regular meetings of his foremen and staff people to get their ideas. Yet he didn't get the job because his *results* weren't good enough,

It went to another fellow who was frankly poor in many of the administrative skills. The successful candidate received few formal written reports. He held conferences less than once a week, and then only when it couldn't be avoided. He had no charts on his walls showing him the level of various key indices. Most of this time was spent out in the plant talking with people, sticking his nose into offices of foremen and offering help when it was advisable. He always had time to look at any new gadget which one of the mechanics had put on a machine. He knew the union stewards and officers well, and chatted briefly with many of them daily. He was well acquainted with all of the employees, and was available for informal chats.

The decision to pick the second man for promotion didn't have anything to do directly with his practices and systems, or lack of them. He was chosen over the other solely because he made things happen. For him the department ran at peak efficiency. His people didn't let minutes slip away from them. If a line or a machine broke down the crew moved quickly to another one and kept working without delay, while the mechanics pitched in to get the first one back in operation. His output per hourly wage dollar spent was more than fifteen percent higher than that of his colleague who was such a fine administrator. His spoilage was lower, his department had fewer accidents, and the number of union grievances filed with the personnel department was zero. Tireless, good-humored, optimistic and knowledgeable, he made things roll along with apparent ease.

Now, what was the difference between the two?

The important variation wasn't the methods they used, and we shouldn't induce from this example that good administration and procedures are foolish. In fact, once the new plant manager took over his job he used them well. The only point here is that there is a difference between *management* and *administration*. This big difference is that the manager makes things happen by whatever means are required, while the administrator follows certain procedures mechanically.

The administrator follows a stereotype pattern whether it applies in his situation or not. The manager sizes up the situation as it exists and decides to do those things which will make things happen whether they fit into the text or not. It's perfectly true that these administrative techniques may be just the ticket in some situations. In such circumstances the manager follows them, *as long as they continue to produce results.* When they cease doing that the manager does something different until he finds the techniques that produce the desired results.

In short, management means making things happen; administration means following certain textbook procedures mechanically whether they produce the results desired or not.

Management Is Not a Passive Art

One of the major complaints of the experts in management development is that too many executives are looking for "a gimmick." James O. Rice, for many years vice president of American Management Association and now president of his own consulting firm in New York, puts it this way:

It's an appealing idea for some managers to think that maybe there is a magic formula which they can apply, thereby solving their problems. I've been in this business quite a few years, and if there is such a formula I've never seen it.

The enchantment of the gimmick or formula, whether it's psychological tests, work simplification, or a five step plan for selecting workers, is intriguing. The big attraction of such a formula is that it reduces management to something which is passive or mechnical. Simply learn how to use the formula, wait for people to bring the problems to you, apply the formula and the answer becomes obvious.

This would be a wonderful labor-saving device, but unfortunately there isn't one such formula worth mentioning. Underlying every successful organization is a corps of hard working people in management and staff position who are actively seeking out flaws and defects which need remedying, and who also fix them up. But there's more to it even than that.

A manager is more than a problem solver. He's a goal setter. Without waiting for others to ask him, he envisions things that should happen, and thinks through some possible paths by which the goal can be reached. At this stage he has few, if any, people who would agree with him that the goal is possible. Because he's active in deed as well as thought, however, he converts them into action in his plan, and enlists their talents toward reaching the goal which he dreamed up. Before long he has a full scale movement afoot and people become ego-involved in his goal just as if they themselves had thought of it. During the struggle to accomplish it, the battle to overcome competition, costs, and other problems in the way, he's there to help. He keeps them pointed toward the objective, and suggests and sets examples of how it can be reached.

Now he may do this by good administrative methods it's true. Being a good manager *doesn't preclude* being a good administrator. It merely implies that he's not a passive administrator who's more concerned with a "clean desk" or proper decor for his office because he's been told that is how administrators should look. Nor is he overly obsessed with procedures for control and review. The dominant trait of the manager who makes things happen is that he's *goal oriented.* It means further that he's actively and intelligently seeking that goal. He's doing more than presiding over a group of people, he's leading them somewhere. Furthermore, while he's doing that the chances are that he's hatching up even more ambitious objectives beyond that one.

One of the spectacular accomplishments of the decade has been the Sylvania Electric Company under the leadership of Don Mitchell as its chairman. When Mr. Mitchell took over Sylvania it had sales in the neighborhood of sixty millions annually with a strong but not dominant position in the electric products industry, especially TV tubes. By 1959 the company had grown to over $360 million in sales and was a leader in certain of its product lines. It merged with the General Telephone Company and Mr. Mitchell became president of the combined electronics and communication firm. The new company has annual sales in its field of over $1 billion annually.

The IBM story of active movement is equally, if not more, impressive. At a meeting of its top management team at Williamsburg in 1956, Tom Watson, Jr., newly elected president, announced the goal of the company as growing from annual sales of $734 millions in 1957 to $1.5 billions by 1962, with an increase of some forty thousand employees in the process. Although it's too early to say whether they'll make it, a report of their current sales and growth shows that they are ahead of this target (1.2 billions in 1960) for the time elapsed since this objective was announced. Such achievements are common in large companies, especially in industries which are growing, such as electronics. Yet other companies in the industry during the same period have not increased at all, and others have gone into periods of decline.

Making Growth a Company Goal

From these examples and many others which are similar a few dominant trends seem to emerge. One of these is that *company growth* is one present day goal which seems to spur executive action and make things happen. This has some important implications for the company which wants to grow. It also has a great deal of relevance to the budding manager—or the one who's arrived—who has talents for making things happen and seeks ample opportunity to demonstrate his prowess along these lines.

Studies by the Stanford Research Institute of several hundred companies with records of growth show that there are several traits which are common to most of them. For one thing they are oriented to growth industries. Not only are the managements of these companies alert to where opportunities lie, they are not averse to dropping lines which are shrinking in market importance and future opportunity. Growth, and management action to accomplish it, are less likely to be found in the hay and grain business, or horse shoe manufacturing than in electronics, missiles, atomic energy, pharmaceuticals or chemicals. Far too many companies fail to grow, the Stanford studies show, because the managements of these companies have a sentimental attachment to products or processes which were once growing and profitable, but which time has now proven outmoded.

Take the case of the large food companies which still concentrate much of their top management time and energy into the flour business. Milling capacity is now far greater than is needed for the production of all the baking flour needed in this country, yet these firms allow the dead hand of the past to rule the future, and as a result channel energies in pursuit of a fading market.

Another food company, less tied to the past, has cast its lot with the newer growth lines—plus bold advertising—and is surpassing its competitors in growth of sales and profits. Needless to say, the latter also has about it the magic to attract the more talented and able young men who seek personal growth through identification with the company's goals of corporate growth.

Stanford's studies also showed that those companies which have growth patterns have been led by management of great moral courage in making decisions in favor of growth and sticking with them to make the growth occur.

> *To summarize this point: action-getting management means more than hustlers in management positions. It means intelligent choice of good goals, among the most prominent being the goal of company growth.*

The Forces of Inertia

More often than competitors or actual opposition from those who have different objectives, the manager who makes things happen finds himself fighting a force called organizational inertia. This inertia takes many forms.

The first is the natural tendency of inertia within the manager himself. The tendency to coast along, or to look back "and see how far I've come" overtakes some managers and they turn into administrators. The truly action-oriented manager seldom spends much time walking around his accomplishments admiring what he's done in the past. He's too often engrossed in getting things moving toward the next higher goal.

Even when he hasn't this inward desire to taper off his efforts, the action getter finds that he has the heavy responsibility for spurring others to overcome their own inertia. This demands that he have several important capacities. He's got to be able to move projects and people off dead center and get them rolling toward his goals. He's got to generate enthusiasm for these goals so that people adopt them as their own, with the result that they generate enthusiasm on their own part for getting there. He must further instill a desire to excel and do the job fully and without mistakes or faltering. To do this demands several traits in the action-getting manager which he must assiduously cultivate at the risk of failure.

1. He's going to have to maintain optimism if he's going to overcome inertia. Most managers who make things happen have ego drives that push them on personally, and unbounded optimism and confidence that others will ultimately see his vision of what's to be accomplished despite repeated defeats and failures.

2. He needs a sound knowledge of people to impel them to produce and create. He needs to know what incentives are required to get action from others, and to have some artistry in using them.

3. He needs a certain callousness in demanding high standards of performance from others who are helping him. The manager with an over-developed sense of sympathy and understanding of failure will usually "usurp all of the dirty jobs for himself while others stand about and marvel at his performance," as David Moore puts it.

One of the greatest wellsprings of inertia in an organization is its *size*. The big organization develops built-in inertias, simply because it's so big. Kenneth Boulding of Michigan University compares the giant corporation to a dinosaur, and warns that unless the big organizations overcome the inertia and ineptness which overtook the dinosaur, they might suffer the same fate. *Power* alone isn't enough to survive. It requires the ability to move with agility and vigor, and to handle a variety of problems, both big and small, which confront the big organization.

A number of things occur when an organization grows in size. The first effect is that communications between the top and bottom, and between the various members, becomes difficult. This means that the left hand sometimes does things that duplicate or conflict with what the right hand is doing.

Another effect of bigness is that the personal touch between the owners and the employees is lost; or in the case of a publicly owned organization such as a manufacturing corporation, between the management and its staff and employees. Since it's this personal touch which is often at the heart of getting action in an organization, the top man finds he is limited greatly when he has a great organization to run, and must accordingly organize to overcome the effects of too much bigness.

Because the organization is big it requires more rule of law (called procedures and policies) in order to govern it. These are perfectly sound things to install, but they are part of that body of knowledge called *administration,* and at the same time they make it possible for managers to function at all, they aren't by any manner of means a guarantee of movement and growth. That happens when the manager in favor of action, makes his personal impact on the organization.

Mr. A. Z. Kouri, formerly executive vice president for consumer foods activities of General Mills, Inc., and now in the oil business, is such a manager. In many respects, his associates report, he ignores the conventional techniques of administration. His forte is strong personal drive and imagination, and the transmission of this enthusiasm and energy to others in the organization. Salesmen in every part of the country for General Mills knew and personally identified with him. It was not uncommon for him to hit a remote sales district in the south early one morning, and start out before breakfast calling on grocers with a salesman. All day long he'd push from store to store, selling new lines and showing the salesmen how to get more shelf space for Wheaties, Kix, and Cheerios. He'd poke his head into the supermarket's stock room to be sure they were rotating General Mills stock. On some occasions he'd take off his coat and roll up his sleeves to arrange a display on the center of the grocery store floor featuring a new Betty Crocker mix. Until late that evening he led that salesman a grueling pace, covering the small stores and delicatessens that are open until ten or eleven. Finally when the exhausted salesman dropped him off, A. Z. headed for a train or a plane to take him to the next town five hundred miles away, where he repeats the performance with another amazed salesman. Some days it's the factory which he tours, or perhaps it's a troublesome supplier whose efforts need bolstering. In any case there's little doubt when A. Z. was there things happened.

To sum up this point: There's nothing about an administrative procedure which will overcome inertia. It takes an action getting manager to make things happen.

Profit Requires Action

Being a successful manager in a commercial and industrial enterprise means a profit-minded one. Conversely, it's the profit-minded manager at any level who stands the best chance of moving upward. This is more than simple avarice, or single minded love of money for itself. It's largely because profit is a universal standard for measurement that is easily grasped by managers and quite clearly understood by those who judge his performance.

It's entirely possible that someday a more commonly held standard will come along, for example—service; but it must always meet the standard which profit has become—immediate, easy to calculate, universally accepted.

Profit, for all the criticisms leveled against it, is the best available instrument and standard of managerial success and organizational performance. With adaptations it applies to any organization, even in Soviet Russia.

We hear a great deal of pious foolishness written and said about profit. At the annual congress of industry of the NAM each winter, solemn and quite pompous words are uttered in defense of this mysterious lubricant which causes the wheels of industry to turn. To some it becomes a divinely inspired instrument which it becomes sacrilegious to damn. This of course is not the point here.

There's still another error which is perpetrated by accountants when we think of profit. It's widely held fiction that profit is something exact and precise which comes without deviation or man-made influence out of the impersonal exactitude known as "the books" of the company. This of course is nearly as fallacious as the assumption of its divine nature. All of the ingredients which come out at the end of the year under the over-all label of "profit" are quite flexible and under the control of individual decisions of managers or administrators.

Such things as expenditures for research, training, public relations, personnel management, and so on are all drains on the immediate profit in the current accounting period. You'll note that all of these are the results of the decision of management to spend money out of current income in order to assure the future growth and stability of the company.

Profit, then, is more than an accounting term. It's a positive creation and standard for measuring effectiveness of management action and decision making.

Let's illustrate this. A large company begins by having some kind of trade advantage—either a patent right to exclusive manufacture of a product, or a dominant position in a market due to aggressive salesmanship. Theoretically each company has such a special advantage which keeps it alive in the face of competition.

Yet companies go bankrupt. One study of the 100 largest firms in the United States in 1927 shows that only 50 per cent of them still exist. In its early days the National Cash Register Company used to maintain an exhibit of machines produced by companies which had attempted to enter the adding machine business and had gone broke in the process. Oswald Knauth, former treasurer of Macy's store, once said that "almost all trade advantages can be duplicated." Except for certain patent arrangements or exclusive access to raw materials there are few advantages which a company can acquire that will preclude the necessity of managers who continue to discover and build up advantages for their own firm through personal leadership. These include actions which will build up its internal and external position, and the development of people, trade connections and experience which results in profit.

The world which Adam Smith depicted of automatic competition, with the functioning of "natural laws" arranging the levels of profits of the respective firms, was never really a picture of life. Profit is the result almost wholly of the *actions of managers* who exercise initiative and leadeship of a dynamic nature, and of the people who respond to this leadership to carry through toward the goals of the organization.

There is probably no company in business today which couldn't be out of business through lack of profit inside of ten years if its management attempted to conduct its affairs simply through mechanical application of administrative practice, at the expense of the more vital, personal, and human application of individual leadership.

The Manager and the World Outside of Business

This individual leadership which produces action and results isn't limited to the four walls or admininstrative boundaries of the firm. Profit, survival, and growth of the firm today—and in the future—will demand that managers be able to make things happen in circumstances in which a lot of the important variables won't be under their jurisdiction. Let's look at a few of them:

- The company which isn't attuned to public opinion is taking undue risks with its future.
- Government actions have a vital part in business policy.
- What's happening abroad is sufficiently close to business decisions today that they must be part of the action-getting manager's calculations.

One of the paradoxes of our time is that the model of manager who is sometimes identified as the "result getter" and the hustler within the business is so engrossed with day to day decisions inside the firm that he doesn't take time to watch these key developments outside.

However comfortable it might be for such an executive to concentrate on the places where his efforts seem to show immediate results, it's highly improbable that he can continue to do so with continued success. It's a further paradox that when confronted with such outside problems as international trade, tariffs, cold war, inflation, and governmental control, he often throws up his hands in despair.

The new action-getting manager must be one who can make his force and result-getting talents felt on both internal and external matters to the company.

As a citizen of the free world he must help preserve that freedom in the light of the threat of the communist world. Allen Dulles, director of the Central Intelligence Agency, has reported to the Congress and public that Russian reinvestment of its national income for growth is proceeding at a rate which exceeds ours by a substantial amount. This brings forth the distinct possibility, Mr. Dulles reports, that Russian productive capacity might well equal and surpass ours by the turn of the century.

In addition to this somber threat, there are the domestic problems of conformity and a deadening sameness in mass culture which promises to reduce people to a euphoric level of TV-bemused idiots without knowledge of the cultures and arts of our civilization.

The problems of labor management relations are also more serious than the loss of profits to workers and company when the process of collective bargaining strikes serious snags, such as a major steel strike. In our highly specialized world the list of what Stuart Chase once labelled the "paralytic trades" has increased. These are the occupations which are infinitesimally small in relation to the whole population, but whose control over some vital aspect of our super specialized life is sufficiently great that public convenience and often public health and welfare suffer when they are stopped from exercising their skills through disagreements with their employers which result in strikes.

Clarence Randall, for many years chief executive of Inland Steel, points to the two major areas confronting American management in the future.

1. The first of these is added acceptance of the responsiblity of business management for carrying out its share of social responsibility in the community in which it works. In this regard Mr. Randall feels that business management has come a long way.

Beyond this Mr. Randall feels that equally responsible behavior by managers must be forthcoming to discharge its responsibilities and apply equal resourcefulness in the face of world problems. He said:

> If we are willing to face outward as well as inward, American free enterprise can become a powerful force for good in the world, and can at the same time assure its own survival.

Good management then means action—and not reaction—to both internal conduct of its affairs, but also action for greater social responsiblity in the narrow community in which it operates—and in the world beyond.

2

The Status Quo—
It's Not Good Enough

"The new American—the child of incalculable coal power, chemical power, electrical power, and radiating energy, as well as new forces not yet determined—must be a sort of God compared with any former creature of nature."

—HENRY ADAMS (1904)

All of the cards are stacked in favor of the man who can make things happen in management. Unlike the stagnant societies where caste and custom, tradition and religion, militate against change at a most fundamental level, in the United States he is rewarded amply for his ability to get things done. Here's why:

● He's working in a climate where economic growth and the growth of the individual firm are considered matters of greatest urgency.

● The history of our country has been one of rapid growth and economic expansion.

● There are legal and social pressures for growth and expansion.

Under such circumstances it becomes a puzzling matter why more people aren't action-getters. Frequently this inertia and inability to make things happen results from the large size of our economy and the companies in it. Complexity, confusion, and delay seem to appear on every hand. How then does a manager orient himself in order that he not be ensnarled in size and complexity? Two ways suggest themselves:

1. He focuses upon growth in the economy and in his own firm as a primary target.

2. He uses the skill of the action-getter to move his organization along this growth line.

Gearing to the Economic Climate

Most Republicans and Democrats alike agree that our economy must continue to grow. An expanding population and a more productive labor force call for three supporting forces to expand accordingly; more employment opportunities, higher levels of investment, and increased consumption.

This growth pattern of the economy is not an automatic process. It is the result of conscious planning and effort, and hard work from many people. The leadership in this growth will be required in many places, including corporations, unions, and in the government.

This economic climate for growth poses some special problems for the manager. It means that when he rests on his oars he will drift backward. If the economy grows at a steady rate and everyone else is moving ahead with expansion and growth, the individual manager can do no less if he would hold his relative position. Let's see how this works out for the individual company.

Productivity per worker is one of the key areas where management must continually improve its performance if it's going to keep abreast of the economy. It's most unfashionable—or perhaps unpatriotic—not to do so. The pinch in *not* increasing productivity is that the competition is probably doing so. This means they will be producing products at a lower cost, and possibly gaining sufficient edge to take over pieces of the market your company now holds.

New capital investment. The company which trims its sails in investing in new and better plants and equipment may find itself noncompetitive with the companies which have not done so. Since the obvious and apparent pattern is one of great capital investment—mainly from plowed back earnings —the company which won't, or can't because of low profit, keep its capital investment up to its competitors will find itself in a competitive bind within a relatively short period of time.

Research and development. New products and improvements of present products are part of the growth pattern of successful companies. Take the case of the large consumer products company which trimmed its expense for research on products for three years in the face of some slight market and profit reversals. During this lull in research on its product one of its competitors pressed ahead and made a breakthrough in product quality and design. With the improved product in hand it poured great sums into marketing the new style and captured more than thirty percent of its one-time dominant competitor's customers. Although the first firm immediately accelerated its development program to catch up, it was too late, and it will require several years and plenty of grief before it can regain its position.

Cost reduction. The need for constant attention to rising costs, and the development of better and more economical ways of doing things points to the cost reduction job of the management. Fat is becoming more and more unhealthy, and the pressure of inflation demands more aggressive and intelligent control over expenses, and positive management action to reduce them.

The Organization at Rest Is Dying

All this proves simply that the company which hopes to survive in to-day's economy must grow or it will fall behind, and probably fail or be merged. There are some very real evidences that this will happen—and in fact has happened.

One of the dramatic stories which illustrates this is the Ford Motor Company story. During the latter years of the life of Old Henry, the company, which had once set the pace for the industry, was losing money at an appalling rate. The methods of modern management and innovation had passed the older management by, and in its resistance to change was draining away its life blood. Henry Ford II, recently out of Yale and with limited experience in the firm, was thrust into the top position. By hiring away such men as Del Harder from the E. W. Bliss Company and Ernest Breech of Bendix Aviation he reversed the trend, and led Ford back into a strong position among the top three.

The strong electronics firms are those which turned quickly to TV, missiles, and other growth products after the war when the radio business was threatened with obliteration. Motorola Company is an excellent example of how one firm can be big and agile to changes in the economy and markets, and use this dexterity in managerial decision-making to gain market position.

One of the great dangers which any manager, at whatever level, can face is the acceptance of the infallibility of past methods. This is especially true following a period of some success. The empty and decaying textile mills of Lowell, Lawrence, and Manchester along the Merrimack River in New England stand as monuments to managements who thought they could live forever on the fruits of dead men's ideas.

Stanford Research Institute's study of why companies grow demonstrated that the expanding companies usually build on a hard core of successful past operations. From this we can conclude that they haven't broken completely with the past, and their future relates to their past in this way. There's a lesson here for the manager in any business at any level.

> *Survival for the company or any part of it means that the management is building on past accomplishments to make it grow.*

Ten Rules for Identifying Business Stagnation

During the depression of the thirties many economists developed a theory of "secular stagnation" which they declared had overtaken our economy. The end of the frontier, the leveling off of population, and the inability of the economy to grow further for these reasons, they declared, meant that greater government investment and intervention to provide jobs for all was indicated.

Since the end of World War II we've heard little of such theories. For one thing population has risen steadily, and the frontier which was the American west has been supplanted by the frontier of research. Through new products, processes, and methods, new employment and investment opportunities have been created with the result that both investment and employment opportunities have been at peak levels.

Yet this specter of stagnation is always just ahead of us in individual companies, or departments of them. Despite the economic forces which make for vitality and growth, there still remains the overbearing necessity for managerial action to make the growth occur. What indicators could we find that the danger point of stagnation is setting upon an organization?

Usually the stagnant organization has ten key characteristics:

1. *Its officials are out of touch with broad trends.* Often the organization at rest is headed by officials who have become inbred within their own company and see little significance in what the economy, or their competitors are doing. Often this state occurs when some slight technical difference in the business from most others, seems to exist. The phrase "our company is different" is often the first sign of decadence in management, since it indicates a general unwillingness to keep abreast of new ideas.

2. *Unwillingness to experiment.* The management which hesitates overly long in accepting new methods or of relinquishing old ones may be headed for oblivion.

3. *It never looks beyond its own markets.* When they run into hard times with product marketing, their only reaction is to mine deeper in the same vein rather than seek new fields for utilizing their products—or their organization—to recoup losses.

4. *It demands great conformity from its people.* The organization which

doesn't allow at least a few mavericks who will question and probe present methods and programs will probably stagnate shortly if it hasn't already done so.

5. *It neither rewards merit nor punishes failure.* The organization which operates with a "civil service" mentality, without paying for performance alone, is on the verge of stagnation.

6. *Managers and staff do little self-development.* One of the benchmarks of the stagnant organization is the managerial staff which makes little or no effort of its own accord to learn new methods, study new techniques, discuss ways of improving, or show any evidence of a thirst for better ways of operating.

7. *It is inbred.* One certain evidence of stagnation in an organization is its isolation from new ideas, new people, and fresh viewpoints. Such a company seldom permits its people to attend professional meetings, permits little exchange of information with other companies, and abhors consultants. The overall climate is one of smugness, self-satisfaction, and self-congratulation.

8. *It is overly obsessed with immediate profit.* A company which is unwilling to invest certain of its present income in enlargement and developmental activity such as personnel, public relations, management development, scientific research, marketing research, or long range investment in intangibles soon begins to show organizational hardening of the arteries.

9. *It attracts passive and dependent people.* One of the surest identification marks of the organization which is on the road to stagnation, if not already overtaken by the dull gray look of mediocrity, is an overabundance of passive and dependent people. These are people who are frightened of the boss, who seek security rather than opportunity, whose principal trait is obeisance not only to orders but to what they *think* the boss would want. Such a climate soon repels the vital and energetic man of ideas and ambitions and he seeks out a livelier and more fertile climate for his talents.

10. *The stagnant company is a boring place to work.* Ruled by seniority, privilege, and low turnover, it has a dull, colorless, and nearly lifeless passivity about it. There is little fire which comes with innovation, change, and the conflict and confusion which comes with growing pains, but which are signs of life and energy. Often it's a humorless place, in which the officials take themselves seriously, and treat restlessness and desire for change as discordant influences which must be put down.

Often the organization which is afflicted with these symptoms can be identified simply by walking through it. There is little of the hustle and burgeoning activity which seems to surround the organization on the move. In some cases it's apparent by the appearance of its managers, who are dull people, and occasionally by its decor which is outmoded and plain. There's little of the stormy, husky, or brawling nature of the broadshouldered organization. It's seldom coarse, strong or cunning in its dealings. Pale and dissatisfied, it stands ready to fall before the company which is young in nature and willing to build and break and rebuild again in the battles of the market place.

Alan Harrington, in his book *Life in the Crystal Palace*, describes it this way:

> I think that our new species may be distinguished from other American working people in at least one way, by an absence of nervousness. We are not worried about our jobs, about the future, about...much of anything.

Why Change Is Necessary

However restful the stagnant organization may appear, the disruptive and sometimes exciting world of change is the route to survival for the well managed company. The favorite cliche of executive speeches, "the organization which is not growing will die," is less fully understood than it might be. In this instance there is some logical evidence which points to the validity of this oft repeated homily. Some of the major reasons for this imperative need for change in a business organization might look like this:

Costs have reached such a scope in most firms that near herculean efforts are required to keep them from running the firm to the wall, if the firm is careless about them. The secular—and constant—trend of costs upward through rising labor costs, rising material costs, the higher costs of government—the only hope of holding inflationary forces under control is the vigorous and active leadership of management. It's perfectly true that this pressure was suspended in large part for many years in its more serious forms through the simple mechanism of shifting the incidence of costs to the consumer through price increases. This circularity in economic management however, inevitably has its bad consequences in inflation which devalues fixed incomes, and did in fact create substantial consumer resistance to further price rises. Thus the only remaining alternative for managements in the face of such pressures—sometimes identified as the "cost-price squeeze"—is to cut other costs in the face of rising labor costs.

Such improvements can only be brought about through better organization, which is to say, changes in traditional and past methods of organization of work. This extends to methods, equipment, rules of work, and procedures. Without such changes in the individual firm, loss of profit and inevitable economic disaster is the only alternative. In the economy at large the unthinkable alternative of runaway inflation would ensue.

Competition of a new order in the economy requires that the firm which would survive make constant change a way of life for itself in all of its ways of doing business. This is most often gradual change, conducted along orderly lines, but often is disruptive in its scope. The newer patterns of lower tariffs has meant that foreign goods may enter the domestic market freely, with their sometime labor-cost advantages, and less often their material-cost advantages. A study of the National Industrial Conference Board has indicated that domestic producers stand exposed to foreign competition when they are capitalized at less than $20,000 per worker. That is to say, for the company which has capital investment in tools and equipment which averages less than $20,000 per employee, there is a distinct possibility that foreign products may be made cheaper and imported to sell at less than domestically produced goods. This too implies that substantial change for cost reduction through better organization and methods must be a matter of unremitting concern to domestic managers.

Not long ago I visited a manufacturer of supplies for the automobile industry in the Detroit area. He has recently developed a process of producing a product which cut labor costs from 34 cents a yard to 8 cents a yard. For the time being, he told me, he was going to continue to sell his product at competitor's prices until he could finance enough of the new equipment to produce sufficient to take over a dominant share of the market for this particular product. It was then his intention, he said, to cut his price in half and grab a much bigger piece of the total market.

"Won't this aggravate your competitors?" I asked.

"Aggravate 'em, hell!" this owner replied, "I'm going to wipe the bastards out!"

This surging rambunctiousness in competition for lower costs and higher quality is not only characteristic of our economy, it is the most cogent reason imaginable for adopting change as the customary way of life for the modern firm.

The Dynamics of Management

The fact of this changing world puts demands upon the skills and practices of management which promise to create a whole new breed of people in charge of our business enterprises. We've alluded to some of the ways in which this new management leadership is different from the "model administrator." The significant differences lie in this desire and ability to bring about change and improvement, and to force innovation into the position of being a primary skill of the manager.

Perhaps the first step in the changing fashion of management will be the decline of those powers which we sometimes ascribe to administrators known as *control* and *veto power*. Study the functioning of the typical administrator in the traditional sense and you'll find that much of his time and effort is designed to accomplish *review* and *control*. Actions by subordinates or other managers are channeled in such a way that they must feed through the filter of the "exception principle." Exceptions, and in some cases routine actions by subordinates, are structured to feed through the mechanism which measures them, stopping them in mid-flight for the purpose of being assessed by the administrator. Those which have conformed to the pre-determined pattern of the administrative directive and procedural instruction are permitted to pass on. Those which vary in the slightest are either altered or rejected to be returned to its originator for re-touching. However laudable this may be in terms of preventing some backward slipping in the organization, it is essentially a provost marshal's approach to management and does nothing more than maintain the status quo.

> *Controls tell what's happened or is happening. They don't make things happen by themselves.*

It may seem reckless and irresponsible to suggest that such controls are not always worth all of the time and effort which goes into their design and operation. Yet, as a major preoccupier of management time they have several basic defects which make them unsuitable in an economic environment where change is so sorely needed and improvement becomes the pressing requirement for growth—and survival. More, there's some doubt in many quarters about the necessity of arming the organization for controlling things when the controls themselves are more costly than the potential losses which could occur from errors in procedure.

Take the case of the firm which found that audits and detailed review of expense accounts took the full time of three people. This was in addition to the time of messengers, typists and the managers themselves in making the detailed corrections which were demanded when an error occurred. A study of the records showed that the total savings over a two year period from this tight administrative control was $125.50. It was decided that two of the clerks could be eliminated, and the time of the remaining one used in simply posting and issuing checks from the statements as received. In other words, the controls over possible padding of checks (which went on, in fact, but this review couldn't catch them) was greatly in excess of any savings that might grow out of the controls.

In many instances such control measures are passed to a computer which performs the calculations, sorts the data and compares it against pre-fed standards and announces the results. Even here there is some question as to whether the computer's time might not have been used more profitably than in exercising *overcontrol* of negligible expenses.

Diametrically opposed in philosophy to this static form of control and administrative practice which serves to maintain the status quo, is the dynamic concept of *action* being the primary requirement of the manager.

A recent example which I saw in a manufacturing plant occurred when a new plant manager took over. As he walked around the plant he struck up conversations with the several foremen in charge of departments. As he went into one department he noted that housekeeping was nearly perfect. The machines were painted, the floor clean, and over the bulletin board was a plant safety award for the best departmental accident record. His assistant informed him that this department was managed by Jim C, who was by far the best foreman in the plant. In production, quality, housekeeping, safety, spoilage, yield, maintenance, and grievances he stood far above the rest. The plant manager sought out this paragon and introduced himself.

"Jim, I understand that you run the best department in the plant."

"Could be."

"What is your accident frequency and severity rate per million employees?"

"Damned if I know."

"Well, what is the hourly average from your machines for the past month and the past six months?"

"Beats the hell outa me."

"And your spoilage rate per thousand pieces for the year to date?" The foreman shrugged indifferently.

"Look Mr. X," he said, "I'm so damn busy running this place well I don't have time to keep score."

Obviously we might want a little more knowledge of the "score" from a manager than Jim C professed. Certainly if Jim is going to move upward he's going to have to learn to use records. The point, however, is that we might also legitimately wish that more of the others, who probably knew their statistics cold, could have Jim's attitude of attention to fundamentals —which was getting things done first, and counting the figures afterward.

No manager ever produced anything by merely watching a figure, and management dynamics emphasizes the doing first, and the administrative totting up second.

Why Innovation Gets Top Priority

Change can be of two sorts. It can be simply the change which comes about because the people running the business can't make up their minds on the best way and keep flitting from one method to another without making real progress. The second kind is based on change which is rooted in *innovation*. This innovation is the process of infusing new and better products, methods, and processes into the concern to do the job better, faster, cheaper. Charles Percy, president of Bell and Howell, reports that 65 per cent of his company's sales are in products which weren't even in existence five years ago. Rather than resting on their laurels they continue to press for even greater advantage through new products. AMA's Phil Marvin reports that in some companies attending meetings of that association there are some growth firms which now account for 80 per cent of their sales with products that didn't exist ten years ago.

"Planning ahead for profits," Marvin says, "calls for dynamic, imaginative thinking."

Arthur Hyde, executive vice president of General Mills for mechanical and chemical division, has said:

"Innovation is the life blood of any growth business. I don't mean just those ideas that come out of the professional 'idea men' in research and development. I mean the innovation in methods that happens when every manager, every staff person, and every employee is taking a cold critical look at his present methods of doing things with a view to finding a better way."

Professor Fred Harbison and his associates at Princeton University have studied innovation and have concluded several things about the companies in which it occurs. For one thing it has a way of changing the personnel make-up of the organization. There usually ends up more high talent, trained professional and technical and managerial manpower when innovation hits an organization. This new concentration of high talent manpower, in turn, because it's been attracted or assembled in a climate of innovation, creates more innovation which attracts more highly trained people.

From this we can conclude that building a strong organization which has the talent to grow and get action for corporate growth is centered around innovation.

John Leermakers, assistant director of research laboratories for Eastman Kodak, points up one significant aspect of innovation which implies that this high priority on innovation isn't limited solely to the research laboratory or the scientist.

"Those responsible for evaluating suggestions for technical work (must) have a clear understanding of the company's field of commercial interest." To this he adds that researchers "must also have a clear understanding of the company's manufacturing facilities and financial resources." Finally he rounds out the picture by declaring that innovation through research must be geared to "the ability of the sales organization to sell and service a new product or process."

Innovation then is a force for improvement through infusing new ideas and products into the organization as a whole, which requires top priority if a company is to grow.

How Innovation and Control Are Related

One of the mysterious features about improvements in management methods and organization is the phenomena which we may call the "backsliding" characteristics of innovation and improvement over time.

Take the case of the typical sales contest. The sales and marketing managers dream up a wonderful plan to boost sales through a giant promotional campaign. In order to cash in on it they announce a contest for salesmen. The winner will get a free trip to Paris, along with his wife, at company expense. Hundreds of other valuable prizes are announced for regional and local winners. Meetings are held and posters tacked to the sales office wall. A monster rally is held and the president himself makes a speech to the entire sales organization via closed circuit TV.

During the months that follow the pressure and hoopla continue unabated, and the red line on the thermometer chart on the sales manager's wall goes up and up until the top is blown off. Salesman Jones is finally announced as the winner, and he and his wife have their picture taken as they stand at the foot of the ramp to the great jet that will whisk them away to Paris for two weeks with all expenses paid.

The following month no charts are kept, and a good thing! Sales have fallen well below the peak of the contest. In fact, it is somewhat below the monthly average before the contest began and even the same month for the last five years.

What happened?

Here the sales manager and his team developed (innovated, you might say) a new idea, and carried it off beautifully, but the slump is worse than anything ever seen.

An investigation shows that Salesman Jones can well afford to take time off for the trip to Paris, because if he were out covering his territory he probably wouldn't get an order from any of his regular customers anyhow. Their stocks and warehouses are piled high with several months' supply ahead, and until the stuff has moved off the shelf they'll be saying "no thanks" to Jones when he calls. Knowing that the contest was a temporary figure to beat, the canny Jones has used pressure and persuasion to get them to stock up for awhile ahead during the contest. Taken on a national scope the contest proves to be a real headache to management and productive of little by way of new and permanent business.

Good innovation has built-in snubbers which are designed to prevent any sliding backward after temporary gains.

This implies some controls, and really pinpoints the place where controls enter the picture, preventing losses and backsliding from the newly won positions.

The kinds of controls which were mentioned in the earlier example of the manufacturing manager who watched his records and ran his department with a view to score-keeping, do then have an important part to play once the organization has reached a new plateau. Organizations on the move seldom take time to dig defensive positions in the middle of their bayonet charge it's true. Once they've achieved their first objectives however, and are pausing to reload their guns before jumping off again, it's wise strategy to post sentries and outposts to prevent loss of the things already accomplished. In management these are the establishment of sensitive control reports and sensing systems to report promptly the first signs of sliding back.

Management consultant Joe Juran[1] summarizes this difference in this way:

> *To establish control to maintain the status quo.* Management establishes norms about which performance will fluctuate under normal operating conditions. If actual performance keeps within the range of expected variation then the situation is under control. Observing performance and checking and correcting variations of results which fall outside the norm is part of routine management control, with maintenance of the status quo.
>
> *Diagnostics for Breakthrough* . . . In order to raise the general levels of performance it takes more than simple control. This requires

---

[1] Speech, University of Michigan, August 1960.

some special "diagnostics," as Juran puts it, to bring about new and different methods or techniques which will innovate and improve upon existing standards.

Once such a breakthrough is established it then becomes time to re-establish control to maintain the *new status quo* at the better level of performance while the next breakthrough is being planned.

Using this viewpoint let's look again at our sales contest and see just what happened.

First, the objective of the breakthrough was clearly defined. The real purpose management had in mind in running a sales contest wasn't just to give sales a temporary spurt. (Although this might possibly be a sales contest objective—to clear the shelves of old stock in preparation for a new item.) Its goal was to raise the general level of sales for the company, permanently, it was fondly hoped by the planners.

Secondly, the entire incentive plan was aimed at causing the salesman to speed up rather than do anything different. The purpose of the contest was to take customers away from competitors and to keep them, once taken. It also hoped to spur the salesman to finding new customers, and to break into markets which had previously not been hit.

Yet the contest merely whipped up enthusiasm for *more*, and with the wonderful reward for selling more so dramatically spelled out, the salesmen went out to sell more in the easiest way, thereby winning themselves a free prize.

Building controls into the contest might have been done in several ways:

1. Make only new sales as qualifying for the prize. That is, sales to customers who were now buying from competitors exclusively have extra value over sales of more products to old customers.

2. Tie the awards to sales of new products to customers who had never bought them before.

3. Run the contest over a longer period of time such as six months or a year. This wouldn't arouse the fervor of enthusiasm of a one- or two-month campaign it's true, but the raising of general levels of sales would have probably been more permanent.

4. More importantly than any of these, it might have been prefaced by some careful diagnosis of markets and sales patterns, and the incentives tied to breakthroughs into new and untapped markets, with no incentives for repeat sales, or extra "pushing" of goods for advance stock to old customers.

5. It might have been supplemented by additional incentives for "business held for six months." These and several other steps which smart sales

managers all know, might be considered as practical techniques for pre-conditioning innovation by building in controls for maintenance of new levels.

Campaigns which are based on pressure, and pep talks that have as their objective the speed up of effort, are always destined to be followed by a let down.

Genuine innovation, based on careful diagnosis, has built in controls to maintain the new levels of performance and prevent sliding back after installation.

The Dynamic Basis for Business Action

Our economy and social system is geared to change and improvement. Each year new models of automobiles, clocks, radios, TV sets, refrigerators, and Miami hotels pop onto the market. The very air seems to create a climate of innovation and change. In such an atmosphere the company which fails to be agile and prepared to leap to better positions, is often left behind. Despite the fact that stagnant organizations are characterized by certain traits and even certain physical characteristics, it's not easy for a company to recognize that it's falling behind merely because it's standing still. This knowledge only has pertinence and meaning when it falls into the hands of a management which can make things happen which will alleviate the situation.

Such managers have two major characteristics. The first is that they are action oriented and are willing to put aside their preoccupation with score keeping when they are in the middle of the contest, and concentrate upon getting things moving and keeping them headed in the right direction. This means that they not only stimulate innovation from the top, but gear the whole organization to accept innovation and create new things themselves. Yet innovation and moving forward requires that the action getter have supplementary characteristics which give him the skill in building sufficient controls to prevent loss of the momentum, and backward movement, once the surge has been stemmed momentarily in order to consolidate the gains.

This double objective of getting action for innovation and improvement, and holding onto them are the minimum requirements of the leader in management positions.

3

How to Identify
What Needs Improvement

*"As any industrial society advances it becomes increasingly de-
pendent upon the brains and much less upon the brawn of its
working forces."*

S. E. HILL AND F. HARBISON

It's said that management expert Frederick Taylor was able to size up
the quality of management in any company by simply walking through
the plant. Self-trained to look for key indicators of ineffectiveness and inefficiency, the "father of scientific management" probably possessed critical
facilities which most of us don't possess. It's also true that his sojourns
through the factory were made on an earlier day when the entire scope of
the business would be encompassed in a single visit or through a single set
of indicators.

Probably the latter day appraiser of a firm would start in a different
spot in his study. In the large and complex business firm of today we'd
start somewhere removed from the plant gate, and track a different course
in identifying possible areas for improvement.

The chances are we'd begin with a look at the attitudes of management
itself. Stagnation in an organization begins with the managment and
extends outward in peripheral rings to its finances, its plants, its marketing
plans, its research and the quantity and sagacity of its staff work, and its
community relations.

For the manager who makes things happen knows how to identify the
areas where improvement is needed. The fact that things have been done
a certain way in the past isn't justification for doing it the same way in

the future. His eye is trained to look at jobs critically, assured before he begins that there is a better way of doing it, a newer system or procedure, or a sharpening of old practices which can be applied. He has a restless desire to see things done better and easier, and he knows that even the best method can be improved if brains and energy are applied to doing it.

He's not particularly impressed by his triumphs of the past, but fixes his eye on the problems ahead. He pictures new markets to be captured, new products to be developed, tested and marketed; and new processes to produce these products at higher quality and lower costs.

For the management with such an attitude of constant improvement the problem isn't primarily one of technique, but first of identifying what particular job, product, or project, should come first. This requires some techniques for spotting what needs improvement.

Six Rules for Identifying Areas for Improvement

Setting these priorities requires some standards for picking targets for improvement. Studies of managers with records of accomplishment in making things happen would tend to show that they usually have intelligence to discriminate between the many types of activities going and focus down upon those that would produce the greatest gains.

Here are six rules for finding these areas for improvement that will get the manager into most of the key areas where improvement efforts will pay off soonest and with the greatest results:

1. *Fix your eye on costs.* Whether the organization is a company which is in business for profit, or is an institution operating with a budget such as a government agency, school or hospital, the good effect of starting with cost reduction is immense. Cost has the quality of being a universal measuring instrument that responds to improvement; in most instances by going down. This doesn't mean that a narrow attention to pennies and the elimination of necessary services is an indicator of good management. It doesn't mean, for example, that you cut away income-producing activity in order to save the money which produces the income. It means you try to spend your cost dollars in such a way that they are producing more service or more income for each dollar spent.

> For example, you don't want to be like the one ice cream company which reacted to a decline in sales by firing its salesmen and eliminating most of its advertising. It means that you take a look at what you are spending and act aggressively to see how it can be used to produce more—or to see how the same volume of service can be produced at less cost.

One paper company during the recession of 1958 attacked the problem of cost reduction by asking every factory employee to suggest savings which would be allocated to advertising and marketing to boost sales and preserve their jobs. The results were a great improvement. Not only did the factory people cut their own cost, but the marketing and advertising staff, knowing that their expenses were coming from pennies squeezed out of operations, worked harder to make them more productive.

The organization which is flourishing and blessed with a rising sales curve and rising profits, may find that excess expenses are less important than getting the goods out and meeting deadlines and schedules. In such periods it's the professional who is able to capitalize on the favorable situation and cut costs.

The *New York Times* of December 18, 1959 reported that even in Soviet Russia attention to cost reduction is getting top priority. Bonuses for workers and manager henceforth will be based upon cost reduction rather than filling production quotas at whatever the expense.

2. *Is it a bottleneck?* One of the key indicators that management action is needed is if one thing is causing delays which holds up several other things. These vital spots comprise a fertile field for improvement since they pay larger dividends in releasing the productive efforts of other machines, processes, or people who have been held up by the offending spot.

3. *Is it taking too much time?* One management man found after some study of his personal time that he was spending an inordinate amount of his time on the 'phone calling and checking travel reservations. By passing this chore to his secretary he was freed for more productive work. The principle here can apply on a wider scale as well. The things which are taking up too much of anyone's time are probably costing more than they should, and are a fertile area for improvement.

4. *Has it drifted imperceptibly in the wrong direction?* One large sales organization found that it had stopped its growth in customers and number of orders from old customers. In checking on the reasons for this declining rate of growth the sales manager discovered that *service* to the customer had slipped in the haste of gathering orders, and a distinct advantage which the company had held in the beginning was sliding away in the urge to get big. By concentrating on reestablishing the quality of service rendered his customers, he was able to start the trend upward once more.

This is all too often true in the organization which starts out with an original leverage in quality or styling, but as it succeeds it lets this original feature go by the board. Such drifting toward the worse can happen without any drastic event to point it up, and when discovered can be a source of big dividends in improvement.

One eastern bakery began with homemade pies which tasted just like mother used to make, and found themselves swamped with orders. As they expanded and went into regional distribution, they hired more bakers and bought more equipment. Without anyone noticing it their pies began to look and taste more and more like everyone else's. One day the elderly lady who had started the company with her own recipe, and was now a director, walked into the board room with two pies. One she had purchased from a company distributor; the other she had just baked in her own oven from her original recipe. Taking out a knife and some plates she served a small piece of each to the officers of the firm. The point became immediately obvious, and a drastic revision in bakery processes took place to get more of the home baked quality back into the product. As a result this company rose to the top in sales.

5. *Have outside conditions changed?* Often the world changes and the company stands still, with the result that the company which was pioneering when it began is now left far behind. Henry Ford pioneered in the manufacture of automobiles of which you could "get any color as long as it was black." This was exactly what the situation called for in his day. Yet after World War II this very policy threatened the company with extinction.

Many companies today have expanded into international operations in an attempt to capture foreign markets. Those companies which continue only to sell their domestic customers often find themselves faced with a statistic of a relatively shrinking market for their products.

Unionization, which has grown from some three million members in the early 1930's to over eighteen million members today, has changed wages, hours and conditions of work in manufacturing industry and many professional service industries. The change in labor markets from one of labor surplus in the thirties to a labor shortage, the expansion of population, the move to suburbia, the decentralization of industry into smaller units of more manageable size, the shortening of the work week for many occupations, all are typical of the drastic outside changes which have their impact on business.

One food company for example has capitalized on the new leisure and higher incomes of people to enter the gourmet food business to capitalize on such a development. Keeping abreast of the gamut of social, political, economic and habitual patterns of consumers is essential in identifying areas for improvement or innovation.

6. *Is it being done the same old way?* In the light of the dynamic nature of business it becomes a fairly safe conclusion that if a job or process

is being done the same old way it was done ten or fifteen years ago—or even last year—it may be ripe for improvement. The facts of innovation and change are that competition in new ideas is increasing and once they've been introduced it's often too late to catch up. Therefore the only safe course is to assume that the other fellow is improving his methods and products, and that doing it the same way year after year is courting disaster.

Cost as a Basic Measuring Instrument

There's no necessity that a manager become an expert in cost accounting in order to effectively use cost as a measuring instrument for identifying areas for improvement. It is a good idea however for every manager, from president to foreman, to have a working knowledge of cost accounting theory in order that he can rightly identify the major areas of cost reduction and cost incidence in his business.

Quite simply put, the cost cycle begins with money and ends with money. There's no secret funds or reserves which can protect a business from ultimately going broke if it doesn't control costs in every aspect of the business. These costs are usually identified as follows:

Prime costs:	Direct labor
	(work done on the product)
	Direct materials
	(materials appearing in it)
Burden:	Indirect labor
	(labor not done on the product)
	Indirect materials
	(supplies used in making it)
	Factory overhead expense
	(utilities, plant management, staff, etc.)
Administration:	General office
	Officer's and staff salaries
	Research
Sales Expense:	Salesmen's salaries and commissions
	Salesmen's expenses
	(car, meals, travel)
	Advertising
	(art, copy, media, agency fees)
	Merchandising
	(display, premiums, etc.)
Profit:	The budgeted surplus which is added to the cost of goods sold.

These terms, which should be as familiar as his own office to every manager, will vary slightly from company to company in terms of how they are defined and classified. Beyond this every manager in the company should be able to identify where the heaviest weight of cost falls for his business and his product. Every manager should know whether or not his business is one which has high labor content relative to total cost, or whether he is in a high selling cost industry. Electro-mechanical products for example are usually high labor cost, where chemical and pharmaceuticals are high in administrative (research) and materials cost. Cosmetics, for example, has its greatest cost incidence in marketing and selling.

Discovering the place where the costs are greatest is a ready-made way of discovering where the greatest improvement is possible. Top management normally begins with a hard look at the profit item, and works back from there. For the directors and officers of the company it becomes vital that this be their major *situs* of attention. Where profit is too low the return on invested capital is lower than it should be, and they must track back through into the other cost areas to discover what's needed in order to improve that picture.

Non-Financial Steps to Goal-Setting

Merely identifying the cost areas isn't enough, however. The means of reducing costs, no matter where they appear, is more than reading a figure. It requires that new objectives for that part of the business be established. At this stage we've left the figures behind and get into the management action phase.

Customarily this involves letting the people in charge of the area where improvement is needed know of the situational need, and getting their active support and efforts for improvement.

In several companies, such as General Electric, Merck, Inc., and General Mills, this takes the form of "objective setting" by top management with the subordinate management of the activity. In Merck, for example, the manager sits down with his subordinates at least annually and jointly they work out a set of objectives which are: (1) organizational improvement, (2) profit improvement, and (3) personal development for the manager. The man and his boss hammer out these objectives for the organization under the manager's jurisdiction, and each retains a copy of the written objectives for the period ahead. At the end of six months, and again at the end of a year, these are reviewed. This comprises the performance review for the manager, and is couched wholly in the terms of his accomplishments against the goals he and his boss have agreed upon.

Within such a framework each manager is made aware of the need for identifying specific things that need improving (including his own personal skills and abilities) and in collaboration with his boss puts himself on record as identifying the areas that need betterment.

This procedure for identifying change is supplemented by the boss asking his subordinate, "What can I do, do differently or refrain from doing that will help you meet these objectives?" This serves to identify the needed improvement in the man-boss relationship required to accomplish the job and get the improvement into effect.

Outside Conditions Impinging Upon Business

Such a procedure as management by objectives works admirably in identifying areas for improvement within the cost structure of the firm. It doesn't always take into account the outside forces which are impinging upon the business that need improvement. Since these outside effects often have a greater effect than internal inefficiencies, they too require clear identification. Unless they are identified before it is too late they may be insoluble problems for management. Let's look at some of the major ones:

1. *The community.* Businesses operate inside the institutional environment of a community. The "community" may be local, regional, national, or global. It draws its employees from the surrounding labor markets, and pays taxes, and obtains services from local, county, state, and federal governments. It also is restricted and bound by the federal government which, under the constitution, serves to maintain commerce between the states and in world trade. This puts the government squarely into the business in the form of regulation, of service, and of advice. Many companies, such as General Electric, have standard forms of "business climate" surveys which cover such things as the general economic health of the community, its educational system, its roads and transportation systems, churches, the availability of airports, and hundreds of other details of community characteristics. These are not forces which are immutable, but can be improved through intelligent business interest and attention to its role as a citizen of the community in which it functions.

Permitting executives to take part in civic and community activities, to hold offices in associations and organizations, to lead civic betterment campaigns, or to go to Washington to hold public positions, are often a result of identifying problems which exist in the community that need good men's effort for solution.

2. *The corporate image.* As often as not this overseeing attention to community affairs grows out of habit or imitation among the majority of

those who participate. Occasionally it takes the form of justification of the corporate activities—"creating a favorable image" in the eyes of the public upon which the firm depends for its survival. Such philosophies are the latter day descendants of the old style philanthropy wherein the economic pirate distributed a mite of his ill-gotten gains to charity as evidence of his basic generosity. While this is less and less frequently true in practice, the experiences of the past are not sufficiently dead for this sort of image to remain in the public mind.

How important is that ephemeral thing which some sociologist has dubbed the "corporate image." As Charles Wade, vice president of R. J. Reynolds Tobacco Company has put it:

> Let us assume that the image of the executive which is widely accepted on the basis of a play or novel, is an unflattering one— that the executive is pictured as a heartless rascal, a greedy grubber after power and wealth, concerned more with things than human needs, more with profits than with persons. Consider then, how the legislator in Congress, or in state or local government will respond to proposed legislation in such areas as tax policy or restrictions upon corporate growth: What will his actions be toward proposed acts to restrain this executive in his control of economic affairs in the market place?

Mr. Wade points out that the inevitable result must be greater constraint upon the decision-making power of the executive. The important point to be made here is that restraints upon the behavior of companies and corporations will hardly be based upon ephemeral images of corporations, but must ultimately be traced back to the behavior of executives. The actions taken by them in support of impingement into business can normally be traced back to their attitudes toward individual managers—especially those at or near the top.

Images and opinions of business which have an all too immediate impact upon their success will be built up piece by piece from the selected images of executives. The world image of the American Business Man is hardly attributable to that godless, soulless entity—the corporation, but to the individual decisions of faceless and anonymous managers. As much can be said for the image of the corporation in state and local affairs as well.

Take the case of the large company in the midwest which announced to the newspapers that it would move all of its plants to another state if a certain rather trivial piece of legislation were enacted by the state legislature. Actually this bit of bluff was the personal statement of its president, issued as the voice of the company. One legislator remarked that the company must indeed be rather whimsical and erratic in its big decisions if if would spend countless millions in moving, as well as sacrificing the jobs of thousands of its employees, in order to have its way in the state capitol.

Perhaps the more fundamental fact is that images are seldom based on press releases, or upon publicity campaigns, but upon solid works and accomplishments in betterment of the community and nation. Even more basic is the conclusion that such actions must inevitably be personal actions by important officials acting both personally and officially. Roger Blough, chairman at U.S. Steel, has expressed it this way:

> Participation in the nonprofit voluntary sectors is further evidence of how the nonprofit and profit are both equally necessary parts of the same culture.

In a free society the corporation and its managers may be unable to survive where too many of them operate on the assumption that they live on an island populated only by other profit seekers. Making things happen in management also requires that executive action be diverted to work with voluntary and civic associations, and the maintenance of quality institutions outside the firm.

4

Overcoming Obstacles

"The world is cluttered up with unfinished business in the form of projects that might have been successful, if only at the tide point someone's patience had turned to active impatience."

—ROBERT UPDEGRAFF

When Ethicon Inc., a subsidiary company of Johnson and Johnson, decided to expand its suture manufacturing and selling operations into a new market, they called in Richard Sellers, a promising young salesman. The new area, they explained, was in Canada, and if he wanted the job he could be manager of the new subsidiary. Sellers leaped at the chance. Arriving in Montreal, he found that he had neither plant, warehouse, nor any employees. On his first night there he was alone in a hotel room, and in his suitcase and sample bag he held the whole Canadian subsidiary of the firm! Ethicon's plants in New Jersey stood ready to supply his orders if he got any, and its management stood ready to back him if he could prove he was there to stay—and grow.

Within two years he had a national sales force selling across the dominion, was selling from his own well-stocked warehouse, and had created, out of his own energy and drive, a whole company which today is incorporated as Ethicon Ltd. Beginning with the thing he could do best—which was selling—he visited doctors and hospitals and cracked a foreign market, in some cases cutting across habits and language barriers that would have stopped lesser men in their tracks. His ability to overcome obstacles led him to the presidency and chairmanship of the parent company before he was forty, and ultimately to vice chairmanship of the parent company of Johnson and Johnson.

Such ability to overcome obstacles is more than a random collection of techniques and routines. It's part of an attitude toward obstacles which prods the obstacle-solver onward to accomplishment of his goals where others with less satisfactory attitudes will fail.

This attitude is the nucleus of actions which prove successful in overcoming obstacles and are far more important than the steps themselves, since the steps are created out of whole cloth in order to accomplish the goal. This attitude, dissected, looks something like this:

1. *A strong goal orientation.* The person who will probably have the greatest success in overcoming obstacles has established some clear cut goals for himself, and is determined to achieve them. The fact that he's faced with the same red tape, difficulties, and suggestions for delay that have stopped others, doesn't faze him in the least. All of these blocks diminish in importance in the bright light of the goal which he has fastened his eye upon.

2. *A callousness to defeats.* The good obstacle hurdler normally has a built-in optimism that makes such things as inertia, opposition, confusion, timidity, and ignorance mere details to be brushed aside or otherwise managed.

3. *Decisiveness.* The most pernicious trait a manager can have when faced with obstacles is indecisiveness. Very often this is explained away as a need for mature consideration of the situation, but actually indecision is the result of the mind slipping away into inappropriate or trivial matters. He may find that ordering a new desk or settling a squabble between two secretaries is much more intriguing than writing the order, or picking up the telephone to announce the decision. The obstacle hurdler makes his decisions when he can—and the sooner the better.

The Qualities of the Obstacle Hurdler

Armed with such attitudes, the obstacle breaker or hurdler has several further qualities which distinguish him from the people who don't make the grade. Most of these he's developed through experience and practice.

Interviews with a number of general managers to discover these qualities show that often he's objective about himself and his qualities in much the same way an actor is. Actors often refer to their bodies as "the instrument" and take calisthenics, or alter their diet or personal indulgences without regret in order to protect the tool by which they practice their trade. This is likewise a characteristic of action-getting, obstacle-busting managers. Not that they pay as close attention to their physique as actors would, since in their case the instruments are different.

The qualities become instruments which seem to characterize obstacle busters and are highly personalized skills in doing things. Occasionally these are closely allied to the actor's, and include dress, mannerisms, and poise under stress. Yet many less successful managers, who have graduated from the right ivy-league school, affect the same manners without having any of the same qualities. More frequently than Brooks Brothers' attire and the other outward accoutrements of success, the quality of *earthiness* in fundamental things appears.

A variation of this is the immense ability to carry details in his head, or a carefully cultivated memory for names and faces. In the early stages of a man's career he will use this facility to amass a great array of names and faces of all levels in the organization. He'll have a speaking acquaintance with as many of the great and successful as he can achieve, and by making sure that it covers a decent spread of those of more lowly station he can avoid the reputation of being an apple polisher or boot licker. Then too, he'll want to make these acquaintances among the lesser ranks, especially among the promising ones, for they may in turn become important.

The executive conscience and sense of honesty is a commonly cited quality for a successful manager, which is perfectly sound for a manager to develop since it helps him overcome obstacles which he might otherwise fail to reduce. Simply put, it eliminates the necessity for maintaining a tangled fabric of distortions or misrepresentations which must be constructed in order to bolster up the first lie. The truth, however bad, is always preferable to the slight lie which looks more favorable since it requires nothing by way of extraneous and superfluous effort and psychic energy to recall in an instant. The manager who weaves a tangled web of half truths or whole untruths must constantly be vigilant to construct a perfect pattern to camouflage his deception. The honest manager may rely upon simple recall of actuality, and finds his mental processes freed for problem-solving and decision-making.

Equally vital among the qualities of the obstacle breaker is that of using people without becoming sentimentally over-involved with their successes or failures. A survey of fifty company presidents by two graduate students at the School of Business at Michigan showed that such things as fraternal connections and other sentimental ties rated last among these executive's considerations when picking men for positions of leadership.

All of these qualities however are subordinate to the manager's ability at problem-solving, of the lock-picking, maze-solving type. This is a function of his powers of adjustment to different and changing circumstances.

Various Ways People Adjust to Obstacles

Adjust he must if he is to overcome obstacles, for problem solving and overcoming difficulties is a process of adjustment that stems from the goals the man has, his urgency in wanting to reach them, and his ingenuity in eliminating or neutralizing the things that block him from his goals. The process for every human looks something like this:

He's driven by the desire for worldly goods, for prestige, for reputation, for self-expression or one of the other multifarious goals that impel people into action. Yet in every day affairs—including those of business—blocks occur. Two people want the same goal which is available to one only. Other people's cooperation is required, and they are reluctant or violently unwilling to offer such assistance. What happens when a goal-seeking man reaches the block is dependent upon his ability to adjust. These forms of adjustment take on a wide range of alternate forms.

Direct attack. Some people find that the normal reaction for them when faced with an obstacle is to lower their head and charge. Where this pattern seems to work for them once they'll try it again. They'll continue as long as it works, and will only try another attack when they finally run into a block that won't topple when it's hit. Since most people run into such an obstacle at one time or another in their life, most good obstacle overcomers use direct attack along with *other* methods of arriving at their goal. Knowing when to attack and when to look for a better way is the first step in adjusting the blocks.

Substitute goals. Another form of adjustment is to replace the goal from which you're blocked with another which *can* be attained. In some cases this may be a goal which is just as satisfactory as the first one, or it may result in lowering the standards of what's expected. While this may be disappointing and even result in a loss of face, such adjustments are often required in business as elsewhere, and the important thing is that the manager not let the fact of having to change goals ruin his ability to adjust well in the future.

Trial and error. Still another way managers adjust to obstacles is to continue a wide range of trial and error responses to overcome or otherwise get around the block. As an example, a general foreman in a large carton factory found that every time he made a suggestion for improvement to his plant manager it was always found somehow to be lacking. If it were the type of suggestion which could be completely reversed, the plant manager seemed to automatically suggest that alternative.

One day the general foreman went into the manager's office to discuss the layout of a new piece of packaging equipment. It was his idea that the machine should be bolted and suspended from the ceiling, thus saving floor space and leaving room for storage under the machine. Knowing that such a novel idea would immediately be pooh-poohed, he fastened upon a scheme.

"One thing is sure," he said, "we don't want to suspend that machine from the ceiling like I've seen some plants do."

"Oh no?" said the plant manager. He then proceeded to berate the general foreman for making such quick assumptions and spent several minutes selling him on his own idea, which if it had been presented as a positive suggestion in the first place would have been given the customary negative treatment.

Perhaps one of the greatest mistakes one can make in adjusting to obstacles is to rely too heavily upon a single response. Efficiency in adjusting to obstacles depends upon the ability of the individual manager to continue varying his responses until success is achieved.

Skill in overcoming obstacles in management requires that the executive become a student of the arts of overcoming blocks to avoid being thwarted by them. For one thing he must know something about the nature of the obstacle. Usually these obstacles to getting what he wants are one of several types:

Environmental obstacles. Those are the blocks which are created by the material circumstances in which he functions. For example, the manager of an international division may find that he's blocked by a shortage of skilled labor in the country. It may be that he's barred from installing some improvement in his factory in this country because the union has a set policy of opposition to changes in work rules or methods. He may find that certain materials or facilities are unavailable. Yet these environmental obstacles seldom are the heart of failure in obstacle solving.

More often he's faced with some *personal defect* in himself that prevents him from attacking the problem properly. Such a defect may be a habit of giving up, or it may be a lack of skill, experience or training in the kind of data that the problem requires for solution. In many instances these personal defects are more imaginary than real, and can be either effectively ignored, or in the case of lack of training can be overcome by hard work and practice. People of little ability are more apt to let an obstacle throw them than people of great ability. These abilities aren't necessarily ones with which the person is born, however; their lack implies a self-development program for the manager as an aid to his obstacle-solving ability. Physical vitality and energy are often at the root of poor obstacle solving, and on more than one occasion a physical check up and corrective therapy has transformed a so-so performer into a successful action getter.

Conflicts of motives are less often, but nonetheless important sources of delay and ineptness in obstacle solving and adjustment to blocks in a manager. These consist of situations in which he finds himself between two desires which are mutually exclusive. The normal desire to live a full family life, and the desire to move ahead in the organization which requires that he give extensive time traveling away from home, are typical of such conflicts. Unfortunately the two conflicting urges don't cancel one another and leave the man bland or neutral. Rather, they create tensions which feed on one another, and result in vacillation and "neutral," non-productive activity. When a manager is split over various alternatives which are opposed to one another, he'll often vent his tensions upon such harmless and useless jobs as cleaning out the files, or dropping into the office of another staff member to pass the time of day. While such actions solve the man's tensions, it doesn't get him over the hurdles which he needs to succeed in his job.

Such words as "worry" and "indecisiveness" are apt labels for the situation in which the manager is torn between desire for the goal and fear of failure, or simple tension caused by the pressures of two strong motives pushing him from either direction.

G. S. Kennedy, board chairman at General Mills, has pointed out that decision-making at the higher levels of management is like walking a girder high above the street. The iron worker is able to walk the narrow girder forty flights up because he has overcome "worry" or fear of falling. The top executive makes decisions which are no more difficult in terms of pure decision making techniques than that of the foreman. It's simply the fear of failure and the enormity of effect if he does so that causes him to tighten up and grab for safety.

Much nonsense has been written about the techniques of decision making as though the failures in this vital area were a lack of understanding of the process. Far more often than inability to handle the data and arrive at the solution, is the fear of failure and the conflict between desiring to get the decision made and that worry about making the wrong one. This puts decision making as an obstacle-busting method into the area of adjustment and only in part into the realm of techniques of collecting, sorting, and analysing data.

Good Versus Bad Ways of Obstacle Licking

This worry and indecision is but one of the wrong ways of adjusting to obstacles. The range of bad adjustments is wide, and the correct ways are limited to those which relieve the tension of the individual and bring him to his goal.

The satisfactory ways of adjusting are those which help the manager arrive at his goal within the framework of the ethical and value systems in which he works.

To a large extent then, the manager who is successful in overcoming obstacles is the man who successfully avoids those things which keep him from achieving it. For the preservation of his ego it's possible to relieve his tensions at levels lower than the goals which he has set. If this weren't true then every person who didn't reach his goal in management—or a satisfactory substitute—would be "off balance" mentally. What are some of the less satisfactory forms of adjustment?

Adjustment by withdrawal. Although there are many occasions in life when the manager must recognize that discretion is the better part of valor, and he must retreat from his stand, this can't be termed unsatisfactory. From the action-getting viewpoint, such withdrawals are merely regrouping for the next attack. Such retreats become unsatisfactory from the viewpoint of management action when the manager never returns to the attack but sits down before the block and vegetates. In some cases he may become publicity-shy when publicity would be the best thing for the situation. In others he becomes timid and respectful where boldness and brass are called for. Occasionally he will plead ignorance greater than he actually should, as justification for inaction. In some instances the withdrawal turns into a form of negativism such as that of the plant manager in the example above. In still others he simply retreats before opposition or even a tough hurdle which doesn't move toward him, but stands implacable and seemingly immovable. In other situations he engages in daydreaming about irrelevant things, but which proves a successful substitute to him for action.

In a medium-sized company in the East, the president was often observed in various forms of withdrawal. The son of the founder, he withdrew into philosophizing about the nature of management theory, and spent an inordinate amount of his time in making philosophical speeches before various management and engineering groups about the theory and philosophy of management. When forced back to reality and the necessity of solving particular problems which were blocking the company, he lapsed into theory. Finally he settled into a highly watered-down version of "participative management" in which he covered his inability to make any decision, however trivial, under the guise of being "democratic." Far from using these instruments effectively, he used them as tools of withdrawal with disastrous results to the company.

Perhaps one of the more interesting forms of withdrawal which every normal person engages in at some time, and which managers do too, is fantasy. This is a form of daydream. Rightly oriented, these daydreams can become the plans for achievement, and are part of the goal-forming process for the manager. The manager who dreams of a new plant may have his fantasy become so firmly fixed that he exerts himself tremendously in order to achieve it in actuality. Such daydreams are a positive aid to the action getter, and he needs a good supply of unfilled daydreams to keep him alive and moving forward.

When daydreaming and fantasy are a form of substitute for actually accomplishing something which he wanted to do but couldn't reach because of some obstacle, then it's probably harmful. These daydreams often run into several forms in their undesirable aspects. The manager may flop in his efforts and retire to his office and enjoy his reveries in which he is the conquering hero. He becomes a great tycoon, or a master builder of industrial empires. Perhaps he pictures himself receiving an award from the American Management Association, or of being invited to be Secretary of Commerce. Occasionally these fantasies carry on through into ambassadorships, cabinet positions, or even the presidency of the country.

If such daydreams are the hard schemes of an ambitious and practical climber they may even come true. Where they are the daydreams of a manager who has just failed to carry off a deal, a merger, or a sale which he had hoped for, they're both useless and harmful. They waste time and dissipate energy. When a manager slips into the habit of fantasy of an undesirable kind he not only fritters away his time, and instead of actually doing, planning, and analyzing which the situation demands, he wafts away into a haze of imagined pleasures and accomplishments.

Adjustment by defensiveness. When a manager hits an obstacle it's also a common thing for him to adjust by building up defenses against the real reasons for his failure. If the results of hitting an obstacle have been especially painful to him it may result in a resolve not to get caught so severely again, and he erects barriers around himself to protect his sensitivities. One president of a small company, for example, led his firm into a new product line quite radically different from the traditional lines it had been in before. The effort fizzled badly, and for many years after that nobody dared mention the words of the product, which had been the focal point of the fiasco, in his presence. He often took personal affront if any slight reference to this product were made in normal conversation with him.

Evidences of this defensiveness are sometimes characterized by avoidance of certain topics or people. One executive who received a slighting reference in a press release one time showed great abhorrence for all newspapermen and press relations after that. Another manifestation of defensiveness in managers is that they will seek out and be overly responsive to flattery. A company officer of my acquaintance, of limited formal education, found that this limitation caused him some difficulty early in his career. By dint of great drive and native intelligence he overcame this handicap and went on past many of his better educated friends. Yet he never fully shook his defensiveness to this seeming defect, and was especially subject to any form of flattery which bolstered his reputation as a thinker, scholar, or well-informed person in the arts and sciences.

For the manager to handle his adjustments to obstacles by establishing defense mechanisms isn't usually a conscious process. Defense mechanisms are learned through blind trial and error, and often grow out of the fact that the manager isn't clearly aware of his own drives in the first place.

Adjustment by compensation. When the reasons for failure to overcome obstacles are rooted in some personal defect in the manager, the kind of adjustment which results in overemphasis of a trait to overcome a feeling of deficiency in it, may occur. The supervisor who really feels inferior to many of his associates may affect a lordly and overbearing manner to compensate for his inward inadequacy. The president of one chemical company was a very short man, and compensated for it by talking tough and acting very roughly with his subordinates and equals. The staff specialist who has few abilities in management may develop uncommon knowledge and ability in one field and thereby acquire status and respect for it.

In some instances individuals who have achieved little in their own careers may become "man-builders" of younger men of greater promise and endowments, and find his satisfactions thereby. Since he wasn't able to lick the obstacles which blocked him from success he adjusts by arming and training others who seem to promise that they can do what he was unable to do. The obstacle is hence overcome, and he becomes instrumental in its demolition.

Other ways of adjusting. To describe these forms ot adjustment doesn't necessarily imply that they are all necessarily bad. There are some forms of adjusting however which are usually unfortunate for the possessor in management since they arouse reaction against him which keeps him from succeeding in future attempts at overcoming his obstacles. *Egocentrism* is such a form. Just as the defensive man may retreat from the press, the attention getter may seek to get his name before the public on every occasion, and retain expensive retinues of press agents to "build up" his reputation. In its worst forms it turns into pathological lies, or self accusations. *Rationalization* is another form of adjustment to hitting an obstacle that stops a manager. The man who fails will go to great lengths to give socially acceptable and rational explanations of his failure. Blaming the tools, the bankers, the workmen, or his luck are such rationalizations. Occasionally this becomes a system of projecting low motives to others, deprecating the goal which he really wants, or more commonly among organization men, is declaring that what he accomplished was "exactly what I had hoped for in the first place." Two danger signs in such adjustment are in seeing conspiracies among others as the cause of his failure, and delusions. The latter two are fortunately uncommon, and are symptoms that the person may be in need of professional assistance in his adjustment problems.

Ends Versus Means in a Free Society

All of this is of course couched in terms of the long-run *effectiveness* with which a manager adjusts to the obstacles which confront him in carrying the organization onward toward the goals he—or others—have set for it. These really are some standards by which the directors might appraise its officers' and executives' ability to get things done for example. Or perhaps it might be a standard by which the vice president of manufacturing judges a plant manager's actions, or a general foreman evaluates the results and actions of his foremen. But they aren't the only standards.

If we were to assume that reaching the goal were all that was required of a manager, then more direct attack, and less of the other forms of adjustment might be expected. Yet, direct attack often leaves in its wake a series of bobbing heads shouting for succor. Under such circumstances the captain of the ship may rightly ask whether or not such expenditures of good people who were unfortunate enough to comprise a block to the action-getting manager, weren't due more civilized treatment. In a more practical vein, the form of action-getting in management which results in a tangled pile of bodies in the slip stream of the on-rushing hero may be the cause of his ultimate downfall and be bad business for the firm. This concern for people, and the dignity of each person—even when he's an obstruction to the path of progress—is one of the underlying values of our society. Because it's much easier to uphold the individual dignity of people who lend us a helping hand than those who thwart us, doesn't change the underlying ethic. The facts are that the end alone does not justify the means used in overcoming obstacles. This requires some further clarification of how managers become obstacle busters, since the *means* must also be measured by several criteria which haven't a thing to do with the virtue of the goal, nor the sterling qualities of the manager who pursues them.

Ours is a materialistic society, and profit, for all of the damnation which has been laid upon it by those not immediately charged with producing it, remains the primary goal of business. The production of great profit has never been damned even by its most vocal critics except as it bears upon the ways in which that profit is obtained. Marx decried profit and surplus as being resultant of the exploitation of the worker. Government committees wield the public interest as a club, and seek to preserve the purchasing power of the public at large through investigations which would induce corporations to cut their sales price for their goods, thereby enhancing this purchasing power. Large profits seem to automatically elicit accusations that somebody is being exploited in order that the high profit was achieved. Despite the possibilities of such exposés and criticism, for the manager it's safe to assume that by making higher profit his primary goal he will please most of the masters whose approval is of greatest importance to him. This, I would suggest is true for *most* managers.

The clear superiority of this goal for management over everything that follows it in rank order doesn't necessarily mean that the other considerations don't exist, nor that they can be ignored. These considerations have to do with the judgments which outsiders will place upon his *means* of accomplishing this end. The manager who makes things happen thus finds himself bound by certain criteria as to means by which he must adjust his obstacle-solving activities if he is to survive. Survival in this instance means that he must circumvent the severe criticism of methods which will loudly resound in the ears of his owners and judges so that it might offset the wonderful effects of his having accomplished what he set out to do.

A. A. Berle, with uncompromising clarity, makes some such charge to management in his book *Power Without Property* when he points up that managers of modern corporations are wielding power without holding property rights to the vast resources they direct. The legitimacy—inchoate if not statutory—of the manager's role, he suggests, exists only because his management is efficient, and *because it takes into account the needs of workers, customers, owners, and the public.* Without the latter considerations, Berle suggests, the inchoate legitimacy of management rights is lost, and he implies that statutory and administrative power will be stripped away in time as a result.

Criticism of management methods as it proceeds to demolish the obstacles to profitable operation and corporate growth take a number of forms. These assume some importance since they automatically—in the eyes of the modern professional manager—become further restrictions upon his methods of overcoming blocks to progress. To clearly understand these criteria it's necessary that management identify them more clearly than being that of other classes of people, as Berle does. It means that the modern manager is constrained from violating certain value systems in which our business system must function if he is to avoid the reverberations which come back to him from his own superiors. These value systems have several facets.

1. *Management gets action inside a human value system.* This human value system in America provides for the dignity of people, respect for their rights to move freely and serve voluntarily in the market place. The use of tangible force is long outlawed. The use of naked economic coercion must be used sparingly in coercing people into lines of conformity with management goals. A hint of behavior which conjures up the image of the corporation with all its economic might, using its power to squelch the economically inferior individual, will always result in strong disapproval from the wider public and ultimately from the owners.

2. *Management gets action within a system of ethical values.* The "new puritanism" of the sixties, growing out of the TV quiz scandals, dishonest advertising, payola, and conflict of interest near the end of the decade before, are but symptoms of an underlying set of ethical standards which existed all along. Management, the prevailing folklore holds, must be ethical and achieve its profits honestly and in a forthright manner. Integrity is a minimum requirement of the manager, and its absence results in retaliatory action by those whose ultimate power is in the political processes which govern all of the institutions and people.

3. *Management gets action within an institutional value system.* The role of free enterprise and private corporations are not only circumscribed by law, but also by prevailing sentiments about them. Managers who hope to accomplish their goals as leaders in such organizations, must recognize the role—and respect it—of other institutions. The labor union, the government, the civic and social institution, the educational system, the church, and other institutions have a status in the eyes of the public. The relation of the corporation to them takes certain broad forms which are really ex-

pectations which the public at large charges them with. For the manager who attempts to overcome his personal obstacles, respect for these institutional values are, by and large, impossible to ignore.

Unfortunately for the manager who wears blinders to these respective value systems, the ultimate power to control his own actions is not his. It rests with government, and under the proddings of a populace dissatisfied with means of management, restrictions upon management can—and have been—imposed without compunction. Often these expectations go beyond simply disapproval of certain practices. They are enlarged to expectations of things that he should voluntarily do. He should actively support the national defense. He should pay taxes without evasion. More than this he should contribute of his profits to educational institutions and of management's personal time and money to good causes. As Clarence Randall has pointed out, he's now expected to take an interest and active part in international affairs of the nation through properly attending to international relations, and behaving altruistically over foreign trade. Such things are part and parcel of overcoming obstacles to business success.

Five Tests of Initiative

"No sooner said than done—so acts your man of worth."

—QUINTUS

One hot summer evening in Hamilton, New York, a group of executives, attending the AMA management course at Colgate University, were having a bull session.

"What's the biggest mistake you ever made in management?" somebody threw out to the group. There were a variety of responses. One fellow had missed a big order because he forgot to follow up. Another had picked the wrong man for a job, and lived to regret it. Still another had recommended the purchase of a patent right which had resulted in a great fiasco for his company. One manager, a general manager for an appliance company, struck a responsive chord.

"The biggest mistake I've made was every instance where I should have done something and didn't. All of the errors I regret seem to center around missed opportunities which I could have taken but didn't, because I decided too late to do it."

Many others chimed in as example after example followed of projects that were half done, or opportunities missed because of that initial step which wasn't taken, or not taken in time.

This process of moving quickly to get things into action is sometimes called initiative. It's compounded of a variety of properties and skills which the action getting manager seems to have that his less effective competitor lacks.

A study of the qualities which go into making up this among men who make things move, shows five basic qualities. These are major characteristics and are compounded of a lot of little habits and skills which the man may have been born with, but most often he acquired them career.

- Initiative begins with inner drive which less effective managers lack.
- Initiative means sorting out the vital from the trivial, and driving for the vital goals.
- Initiative means that its possessor is tough minded.
- The action-getting manager instills a desire to excel in others in the organization, and releases their initiative as well as having it himself.
- The result getter initiates intelligent action—not just random activity.

Only a few of these qualities are innate or natural. The rest are acquired, and can be taught to others.

Men need to have them or develop them if they are to cope with two major forces that are pressing on management today: the larger size of companies and the wide range of problems a manager must cope with to keep abreast.

As companies get larger they run into what Prof. Kenneth E. Boulding of the University of Michigan has called the "scale barrier." This invisible threshold, a little like the sound barrier in flying, seems to stop programs from moving along, plans from being carried through, or the word from geting down from the top. As a result of this invisible wall, which takes the form of procedures, regulations, and plain inertia, a lot of solid administrators in top spots get stuck on dead center when it comes to results. Staffs get so tied up in clearing every decision and writing memos that they don't quite connect fast enough to capitalize on profit opportunities.

Let's look at each and see how the men who make things happen overcome this obstacle and how we can learn to be like them.

Inner Drive

Some people with this trait are endowed with an over-active thyroid, or an abundance of animal energy, but this isn't always the case. The big difference isn't mainly physiological. It's a habit of vigorous and positive approaches to everything, of restless unhappiness with things as they are, and a roving eye toward the possibility for improvement.

The doer has developed the talent for picking a single goal out of the millions available and mustering all his talents, knowledge, powers of persuasion, and leadership to reach it.

He may pause while he's choosing a plan or mapping his strategy, but, once it's selected, his energies concentrate in a controlled form of organizational fury. More than simple activity, it is directed energy guided by an intelligent and well-disciplined mind.

Building or training this inner drive into a man isn't done through pep talks. It's a combination of coaching the man to peak personal effectiveness in his daily work habits. When he's reached that level, the next step is to give him big challenges which test and prove his skills.

Pick the Important Things

In terms of skills which a manager can develop to function as a result-getter, one of the key abilities is to pick out the important things for action. The doer's desk gets piled with the same assortment of trivia as yours and mine. He gets as many requests for his time. He is invited to as many meetings and has as many opportunities to dawdle as the next fellow.

The first step in becoming an action-getter is to learn how to wade through the underbrush to find the really important things and do them first. This means that he has mastered several difficult steps along the way.

He has trained himself to scan the whole range of things that are pressing upon him and quickly evaluate the importance of each. One executive, for example, gets ten requests for speaking engagements weekly. Rather than turn them all down, or accept them all, he measures the effect they might have on his other goals.

He might, for example, pick one with a small group of investment analysts if he's planning to go to the security markets soon. He might talk to an education group if his company is about to launch a recruiting campaign in the colleges. If community relations is a problem, he may accept chairmanship of a fund-raising drive. He may address a group of professional men if his company has market interests among them.

His power of adroit selection tells him which meetings to miss, which conferences not to attend, which visitor not to see, and which letter to buck to somebody else to answer.

He knows that everything he could do is not equally important. Because he knows this, he digs for the vital things. He looks for bottlenecks that will hold up a lot of other projects and breaks them. He puts the vital few things at the top of his list and pushes the many trivial ones to the bottom.

He's profit-minded and he pounces quickly upon things that might increase profits through immediate action, and will prevent loss if done without delay. He then uses this priority list to shuffle his schedule so that the essential gets done now and lesser priority items later.

He's quick to spot a trend that requires some action. If he sees that relations with a big customer are sliding, he doesn't wait to see what happens next. He starts an immediate action program to get things corrected so that the cause of the discontent won't recur, then goes to the customer and tells him what's happened. Most action-getters have two traits:

First, they more often than not go to the top man in the customer company—at least as high as they need to go to set things right. As one such executive put it:

"I find it better to deal with the chief of the tribe than with one of the Indians."

Second, they are not afraid to admit their own mistakes and failure.

The important point again isn't that we must have a natural whirlwind to start with. Everybody has capacities which he may or may not be using. Guided experience and coaching in sorting out the facts before making decisions, and an opportunity to practice in real situations, is the key training method.

Tough-Mindedness

Despite his concern with meeting the needs of others and meeting the basic needs of people, the action-getter has developed a tough-mindedness. For one thing, as Chris Argyris, management researcher of Yale, has put it, he has "a high tolerance for frustration." He can plug through all sorts of red tape without blowing his top when he has to. He frequently endures the delays and runarounds of committees and clearances with spartan endurance. He is patient where such patience is the only possible way of getting the final payoff that he seeks.

This patience isn't submissiveness, however, and when the time for patience is past and more direct action is called for, the action-minded manager is willing to be ruthless. When the choice is between maintaining old relationships and getting the job done he is always ready to decide in favor of the job. Stepping on people's corns isn't his first choice, but he does it firmly if the occasion demands.

One executive found that his plan for a marketing campaign violated certain canons of taste and preferences of his boss's wife. Wiser heads and politic minds advised him to drop it and choose another. After weighing all the factors he finally went ahead. When the results were outstandingly successful his boss confided in him that, despite some troublesome moments at home he was personally pleased that the executive had decided to go ahead with the program.

This tough-mindedness sometimes looks a little like inflexibility. Once he's decided what action is best, he'll stick to it no matter how the weather blows. This is partly because he's constitutionally dogged, but mostly because he knows that vacillation will be worse than picking a specific tack and holding his bearing. He knows that pressures for change are inevitable no matter what course he sets. He accepts them as part of the price for making headway.

The action-minded manager is probably tough-minded in his relations with people, too. He's willing to stick by his people through their honest mistakes—or to chop off heads as the need arises. He assumes that men are made of tough stuff and will work hard and take heavy blows as a price of making a living and contributing to the success of the business.

He will urge on a man who is working at less than his best abilities.

He is liberal with recognition for good work, and equally liberal with a reverse kind of recognition for the people who aren't performing up to their capacities. People over their heads in their jobs find this action-minded man a fearsome figure, one who will certainly drive them to perform things they hadn't thought possible, or face up to the fact that they have no great future in the organization until they do.

He's tough-minded, too, in being willing to pay the prices for personal success. Long hours, hard work, and man-killing travel schedules are the way of life for him. He concentrates on his job with a fury and singleness of purpose that reduces other things to a lesser role. This doesn't mean he's inhuman or a dull grind. His pleasure and his recreation are often found only in work. As one such executive put it:

"I think people in positions like mine have found a secret weapon which really isn't a secret at all—we don't quit. As I look back over forty years and see the fellows who didn't go as far as I did, I think it's probably because they took a good look at the price you pay in family life and so forth, and decided to settle for less. I can't say they're wrong, it's just that they didn't make the same decision I did. They were willing to let themselves be outworked. Add a little luck to that, and it's a secret formula."

How do you get all of these qualities? First, they aren't learned in a course. They are learned in tough situations. This becomes a matter of assignment of men to places where they take pressure. Ford, General Mills and other companies now believe that the best place to start a young trainee of great promise is on a job. It's there that he'll develop the calluses that make him a tough, resourceful manager at 45.

In developing the men who make things happen, major emphasis, it would seem, should be on careful selection of people who are willing to pay the price—people with hides thick enough and frames sufficiently durable that they can learn by being tossed against problems bigger than themselves.

Although conferences and courses can help, most observers agree that major emphasis should be on systematic coaching and carefully planned job assignments. In essence, a program to produce a manager who makes things happen must grind in some habits. The ingredients in this program will vary to meet the needs of the man but they will include:

- Early identification of the people who have the native equipment. This isn't much different from what we're doing at present.

- Assignments that give him these three major advantages for development:

1. Tough problems to solve and big jobs to do where he can see the results of good—or poor—performance early.

2. Assignment under an action-getting manager. One action-getter can strike off several copies of himself. If several go-getters are assigned to an action-getting manager, they'll strike sparks off one another, too. Healthy competition is a good force for bringing out the "will-do" factors and causes people to bring out their best abilities.

3. Work with the manager to help him coach and guide these people.
Once you've got an action-getter in a spot where he can do some good for the company and develop his own talents, get out of the way and let him move.

Instilling a Desire to Excel

The action-getter can use initiative because he's done most of the ground work in advance. He knows that nobody in the company, especially himself, has all of the good ideas. He builds a climate in which a good idea will get itself into application without a great deal of clearances and approvals all up and down the line.

In one large company a staff department was sagging badly because of the bottleneck at the top of the department. The staff, whose job was to develop new ideas for use in line departments, was in a state of near standstill. A close check by an executive found that every new idea or plan which was developed in the organization was being sent in memo form to the man at the top. After doing all of the necessary preparation and careful scrutiny of it for possible points of criticism, it was common practice for everyone to then type "first draft" at the top of the first page before sending it to the boss for approval and checking. Since he inevitably found things in these recommendations which he would alter or change around, no completed staff work was ever done in the department.

When this procedure was pointed out to him, he began to route the "first draft" papers back with the note:

"Don't send me first drafts, I want your considered judgment and recommendations for action."

After several came over with only half the work done (the expectation of the originator being that changes would be forthcoming), the department head wrote:

"If this is your best judgment—let's go ahead and issue it *over my signature.*"

The result was an immediate and drastic improvement in the volume and quality of work in the department. He soon learned whose work he could rely upon, and whose would need some improving through coaching.

All this implies that the action-getter is more than a self-appointed genius who swings his weight around to get people scurrying. He gets them to initiate by making certain they are ready and able to start things in motion. He does this by listening patiently, asking questions, probing deeply into half formed ideas to help the initiator develop them more fully. Not only that but he makes it worthwhile for a man to excel in his job, and to pay dividends for people who move quickly and skillfully in their job. When he sees a half-baked idea he doesn't kill it summarily but listens to hear the whole story. If it's off the beam he explains carefully to the originator why it can't be used. If it's good he gives the initiator sincere credit for having thought of it and put it into application.

He's probably created a climate in which people are scrambling hard for new ideas and better ways of doing things. He's also made it plain that he's tolerant of mistakes, and won't hand a man his head for the first or even the second one. The organization which is initiating ideas will have to make some errors in judgment. They aren't afraid to generate and try out a few of their own. They know that an occasional mistake won't cost them their scalp.

This desire to excel—so difficult to achieve—lies under the whole idea of initiation. It presumes that ideas and excellence grow out of making each person responsible for the results in his own area. Decentralized companies such as General Motors, Prudential Insurance, Ford, Du Pont, and Borg-Warner, with their great records of growth, have generally found that this desire to excel in every level of the organization is what keeps them out in front.

The interesting part of such growth is that it hasn't in many cases de-

creased the agility and vigor with which the organization tackles its problems, not its speed in solving them. The small company which is domi-
nated by one man is often slower than the corporate giant. This deeming
unomaly grows out of the place where initiative rests.

*As a rule, initiative in an organization should be pushed down to
the lowest possible level where decision can be made through
instilling a desire to excel at every level.*

Initiating Intelligent Action

Simply getting the ball in motion isn't enough. It requires *intelligent*
action if the best results are to be achieved. This requires two things:

- *a goal* which is realistic, attainable; at the same time it's hard
  enough to attain that it challenges people.
- *a plan* which spells out in an orderly fashion how the organization
  will arrive there.

This requires more than simply getting things into motion. It means
movement toward the objective. Managers who have "initiative" or the
ability to start moving, based on emotional drives or instinct, won't be as
successful in the long run as the one who acts upon reflection, thought,
and conscious planning. A lot of initiative is based on such instincts and
reflexes, which sometimes leads to self-cancelling or inconsistent action.

There's a metal working plant in the east where the top man has created
a climate of reflex and instinct that isn't paying off. Every time there is a
production stoppage, everyone in sight rushes to the spot and, as one of
the workers put it, "all hell busts loose." Mechanics work under pressure,
and do a slipshod job. Foremen get rattled and bawl out operators and
mechanics. Inspectors and foremen tangle with angry words if the shut-
down is for quality.

The best kinds of initiative are those which are based on experience, and
pre-planned procedures. *Pressure* alone isn't properly showing initiative.

Another key ingredient in intelligent action is taking initiative that will
carry the unit or department toward the larger plan for the whole company.
A plan which makes one department look good at the expense of another,
or adds to another department's cost isn't good initiative.

The following case illustrates the crafty type of initiative which doesn't
do the overall organization any good. It's from *Time* magazine of July 29,
1957.

"The dominant theme of Soviet railway transport policy" writes one
expert in the jargon so dear to experts, "has been that of maximiz-

ing the volume of services provided while devoting the minimum possible resources to them. As freight traffic manager on the Vladivostokection of the Trans-Siberian Railway, Comrade Vorobiev was a man with a mission to fill, and the imagination to overcome obstacles. His job was to move a specified tonnage of freight. But what if there was not enough freight to move? The latest issue of *Gudok,* the Soviet railway journal tells how Comrade Vorobiev met his problem.

In 1955 traffic manager Vorobiev's line was in grave danger of falling behind its monthly norm in tank car loadings. Desperate for something to transport, and finding no petroleum, alcohol, milk or other useful liquid available, Comrade Vorobiev gazed about him, cast his eye upon the liquid in a nearby river, and quick as a flash filled 50 of his cars with water and sent them rattling off from Voroshilov. At a siding of the Trans-Siberian line the water froze solid in the cars and it took a month for workmen to chip it out with pickaxes. But no matter—Vorobiev had made his quota.

Part II

GETTING OTHERS TO ACT

"I believe the greatest assets of a business are its human assets, and that the improvement of their value is a matter of both material advantage and moral obligation."

—CLARENCE FRANCIS

6

Getting and Using the Ideas of Others

"The trend in America generally, in our schools, in our homes, and in our communities is toward giving the individual greater freedom and initiative. There are fewer direct, unexplained orders in schools and homes, and youngsters are participating increasingly in decisions which affect them. These fundamental changes in American society create expectations among employees as to how they should be treated."

—RENSIS LIKERT

Henry Ford was asked one time what he expected of his workers. "We expect that our workers will do the work that is set before them," Mr. Ford was reported to have replied. While this was a perfectly typical method of getting results through others in the early days of the assembly line and of scientific management, it's no longer true of today's business. It has changed in that management expects more of its workers than doing simply what is put before them. It has also changed in that the workers expect that more can be had from them than simply putting in of labor according to the directions of the boss. The worker expects that he will be asked how he feels about his job, and for his ideas on how his work can be done more easily, better, faster, and smarter. A number of reasons account for this change in emphasis.

1. The definition of "worker" has changed. Today there are more professional, technical, and white collar people employed than there are factory workers. The number of unskilled workers has declined steadily. During the depression it fell by some 7 per cent. During the decades that followed the depression decade of the thirties it fell by some 30 to 40 per cent. This downward progression in the ranks of the unskilled man

who has his work set before him according to the plan of a master-mind will undoubtedly continue in the future. Such changes in the composition of the work force toward professional and white collar work means that the emphasis is upon ideas, and creativity from each individual rather than specific performance of engineered tasks.

2. The social values of our society have changed. The child, the citizen, and the employee have been conditioned to receive explanations of the purpose of their work. They have also become accustomed to the environment in which their own ideas and suggestions may be incorporated in the actions they are required to take. This transformation in the overall society has had its impact on the work place. Each person wants to feel that his opinions about the things he does are worthwhile and wanted by those who direct him.

3. Business has discovered that there are tangible business values in soliciting and using the ideas of people at all levels in the organization. The improvement of the value of the people in an organization becomes a strategy for business growth and profit, as well as a socially desirable goal.

The implication in these changed conditions is that there is no corner on brains in an organization. The concept of the single thinker at the top, surrounded by peons who execute his brilliancies has no longer any merit in fact, and tends to arouse hostility and resistance where such a condition is implied through the policies or supervisory practices of management.

Competition between organizations is most often a competition in the realm of ideas, far more often, for example, than competition between accumulations of money, or patent rights.

This competition is obvious to the salesmen for the various firms who call on the same purchasing agent. They see the competition, and know directly the effects of better products, and more adroit choice of marketing methods. While less obvious, the competition is nevertheless just as vigorous between all other people in the organizations who make and sell in the same markets as well. The foreman of company A is in competition with the foreman of company B, as are the secretaries, clerks, and engineers. The fact that they don't *see* their competitors doesn't lessen its effects in the slightest. It's a competition for ideas, and excellence of performance, and ability to keep costs within limits.

Such emphasis upon ideas and the nourishment of them will not be abated in the least by the trend to automation and such new management tools as data processing and electronic systems for handling information. As C. E. Knight and C. H. Falkner of Monsanto Chemical describe the impact of automation on company organization:

Paradoxically, the trend toward disappearance of direct human contribution to product creation will be accompanied by an increased need for recognition of workers as people and more tolerance for the constructive nonconformist.

How Participative Management Works

Tailoring this general philosophy of willingness to let employees participate in the decisions that affect them is easily misunderstood. Often it's construed as meaning a form of "softness" and sentimental democracy in which the boss asks workers permissions before making decisions. Such a system obviously has extremely limited uses, if any, in a business organization.

Yet we know that exactly this "soft" and permissive approach is what is required to make anything happen in voluntary associations where people work of their own free will and for sometimes whimsical motives. The social club, the service club, the church organization, and the professional organization run by volunteers are led by people whose leadership rests wholly upon the willingness of the governed to assign leadership powers to their leaders.

In a business organization the work contract implies the power of the management to hire and fire and otherwise direct the operation of the resources of the company. The principal difference then becomes that in voluntary associations one *can't* act in a certain arbitrary way against the collective will of everyone who must do the work. It's suggested here that in business where you *can* it's often wise not to do so. The reasons have little to do with the moral or social rightness or wrongness of such autocratic behavior but rather with its soundness as a business strategy.

Participative management, even in such circumstances, still doesn't indicate that the management becomes so passive that it abdicates its principal requirement—which is to lead. The role of leader in the group is a real and necessary one, which is recognized by the group. It does mean however that certain actions which give workers participation in the decisions and plans of the organization will make that organization more profitable, efficient and stable. More importantly it can help the organization prosper and grow.

These techniques can be identified in one of several categories.

1. *Good participative management is tied to incentives.* It makes it amply clear to people that their ideas are wanted, and the more tangibly that is made known the more clearly this management interest in new

ideas is accepted and believed by people. Suggestion plans which give cash awards for productive ideas are but one of the several variations of this principle.

2. *Good participative management gives people personal satisfaction.* In addition to the tangible rewards for ideas, workers find great satisfaction in identifying themselves with improvements in their own working conditions. As one factory worker told me:

> I suggested a new layout of the time card and time clock system to prevent the big lines and delays in getting in and out. It was adopted, and I still get a little kick out of seeing people pass in and out without delay or tie-up because they adopted my idea.

3. *People are better team players when they are made to feel that they are important parts of the organization.* Good participative management reduces the helplessness and latent hostility which people feel toward an organization in which they are considered "lost" or simply a number. Even large organizations can permit people to feel that their individuality and special qualities are important if they are consulted and asked about what should be done. In a large meat packing company one driver of a company fleet vehicle told me:

> This company makes its drivers feel like important guys. They ask us about our routings on over-the-road trips. They let us tell them how long it will take for long trips. They explain about the importance and value of the stuff in the load, and why deliveries are important. I pull out of the garage with several thousand dollars worth of stuff on the trailer and I can feel the weight of my responsibility setting in. I want to deliver the goods without mishap.

4. *People should grow in knowledge and responsibility.* Good participative management should be an educational experience for the people making the suggestions. Even a suggestion that can't be used gives him some insights into the overall company problems. An engineer in a pharmaceutical plant suggested that a new evaporator be purchased. It was turned down with a complete explanation. Yet the engineer didn't seem put out. He explained it thus:

> I learned that the average life of a product in this industry was only 1.3 years, and that the product I wanted to improve the process on was already on its way out in favor of a new one which was being tested in the development lab. They taught me something about this business I didn't know because I put in that suggestion. If I'd been in their shoes I'd have turned down my idea too.

5. *Participative management should be a means of identifying people*

of above average abilities. In a climate where new ideas and comments about the job are welcomed, the opportunity for evaluating people's potential becomes easier. If participative management works well it may go a long way toward screening out the exceptionally talented people. Good ideas, not only about the overall performance of the organization, may uncover individuals who think bigger than one might suppose from simply judging their day to day performance. It can be a tip-off on people with inventiveness, imagination, and exceptional ability to manipulate ideas and facts to come up with new combinations.

6. *Participative management should let off pressures.* People who have some gripes or major grievances against the way things are run will ordinarily not let such things convert into long standing and pathological hostility if they have an opportunity to get it off their chest, and see it corrected early. Dissatisfaction among the worker group held down, can lead to big blow-offs and mischief later. Good participative management taps it often and early.

> In a large eastern city a laborer from a factory was arrested for slugging his plant manager with a pipe outside the plant, while under the influence of liquor. Asked why he did it, the worker at first pleaded intoxication, and later confessed that he had harbored a grudge of many years against the manager because he "walked through the plant and never talked to anybody."

Obviously such cases aren't typical in their drastic consequences. It's typical, however, in that aloofness and unwillingness to exchange amenities with people breeds great resentment, and especially the unwillingness to listen.

Learn to Listen

Getting and using the ideas of others obviously means that there is communication with employees. It also means that effective listening takes place, a skill which is not as common as we might be led to suppose.

> "Most of us have a filter which we keep constantly in place when we are listening," says AMA's Harold Schmidhauser. "That filter is a trap for ideas that might have gotten through to us if we'd let the filter down. In most people that filter is simply *attitude.*"

Take the case of the engineers who were laying out a tank house for a chemical plant. The house was to be twelve feet square, of brick construction, and was to house a tank seven feet in diameter. The liquid in the tank would be piped to several adjourning buildings by a pump. One of the laborers in the yard happened by, and looked over the shoulder of the engineer at the drawing he held spread out before him.

"Better make the door a little wider," he suggested. The engineer looked at him as if he were some form of interloper and shrugged his shoulders.

The laborer shrugged his shoulders too, because he'd noticed that the door on the plan was only four feet wide and the tank to be installed was seven feet in diameter. Sure enough, when the building was completed they had to rip out half a wall to install the tank.

In another instance a truck driver, for an over-the-road trucker, was given a route by his dispatcher.

"Now follow this route!" he was directed.

"But . . . " he began.

"No buts. We'll decide the best route from now on," the dispatcher stated emphatically. The driver shrugged and took off down the road. He knew that he would shortly come to a low overpass which his trailer couldn't get under. After waiting a couple hours in a nearby coffee house he called the dispatcher and explained his reason for delay. Naturally the dispatcher felt cheated that he hadn't been told the thing he wasn't prepared to listen to.

Bad listening falls into several types.

1. We're naturally bad listeners because we're preoccupied with ourselves and our own ideas, and this filters out a clear reception of other's ideas.

2. Because most people speak slower than the ear can handle what it hears, there's as much as 50 per cent of our listening time which is unused. This gives us time to let our minds wander. Often it never gets back to what is being said. Most people can hear and understand 400-600 words a minute. The average speaker ordinarily uses a rate of 200-300 words a minute. This differential causes a tendency to let our mind drift away. This is especially true when we think we know what the person is going to say after we've heard a few words.

3. One of the causes of bad listening is that we tend to generalize to the person's ideas something about the person himself. If he uses bad English or has annoying appearance or mannerisms, we are apt to throw out what he says. Good listening starts out with the assumption that there's a nugget of a good idea in every suggestion.

4. We listen passively. Good listening requires sharp attention and active interest. This means that we not only hear with our auditory sense, but watch for facial expression and evidences of attitude. Often the

person speaking is saying one thing and implying something else which is far more important. Here's how one labor relations manager put it:

> Most of the grievances that we get at step one really aren't actual statements of the real gripe at all. The foreman acts high-hat with everyone and the boys in the shop are unhappy about that. They can't file a grievance over that so they scratch around and find something else, something that violates the contract, and they grieve about it. When they get to my office I listen carefully and probe a little and more often than not find out I can get to the real root of the problem.

5. The best listening is for *ideas* not facts. A study by Dr. Ralph Nichols of the Department of Rhetoric at the University of Minnesota showed that the student who listens for facts generally makes poorer grades than one who listens for ideas. This becomes even more important where getting ideas is the first purpose of listening.

6. Listening means *relating*. Good listening means that as ideas and facts come in through the auditory sense they are classified and compared against what's already there. They are then compared, and weighed for accuracy, usefulness, and pertinence. Often they can be handled critically and with completeness. Where the facts or ideas are sketchy a pointed question will bring out the answer to the inconsistency.

Some Devices for Springing Other's Ideas into Action

Research at Cornell University has shown that managers and supervisors spend between 1200 and 1500 hours a year meeting and talking with people—including listening to them. Making the most of this time in getting the benefits of good listening and obtaining employees' ideas, takes some definite steps. Professor Earl Brooks of Cornell lists ten steps which will make such contacts pay off:

1. Listen with interest and sincerity and friendliness.
2. Make the employee the central figure.
3. Recognize your own prejudices.
4. Be careful in giving advice.
5. Recognize that people hear what they want to hear.
6. Listen to understand, and make that your one purpose.
7. Be sensitive to his feelings, attitudes, and motives.
8. Respond in a neutral manner.
9. Repeat or rephrase something he has said.
10. Use questions carefully.

These methods go a long way toward proving to the worker that you are genuinely interested in his ideas. Gordon R. Taylor, the sociologist, once said that people by and large have a desire to cooperate with management in accomplishing its goals if they are convinced that their purpose is a good one, and that the leaders deserve to be leaders. Such devices and habits can help achieve that feeling. Yet there is more.

How, for example, can we be assured that workers and employees at any level will be capable of generating good ideas for innovation and improvement?

The tube department of RCA, in Harrison, New Jersey, has provided for this through a continuous series of training sessions in work simplification which are designed to tap the pool of ideas latent in every employee. Manager, engineers, staff men, and machine operators have all been through this course under its director, Walter Hoffman. Basically the program teaches a five step plan which any operator of staff men can apply to his own job or any other, and come up with ideas that cut costs, eliminate waste, and make the job easier, safer and more productive. This plan is:

Step one: Pick a job to improve. Start with your own job or any job that is costing too much or is inefficient.

Step two: Study the job in detail. Put all the facts down on paper. Make simple flow charts or diagrams. Show distances traveled, weights lifted, etc.

Step three: Question all the details. Ask the five questions: *why* is it necessary; *when* should it be done; *who* should do it; *where* should it be done; and finally *how* should it be done? The ultimate question to ask is: Is there a better way to do it?

Step four: Develop a better way. If the person doesn't find a sound answer to any of the questions about the details of the job, he or she is to figure out a way of doing it better, faster, cheaper, easier.

Step five: Install the new method. Once the new method is mapped out, try it for practicality. Sell it to others, the boss, the industrial engineers, and start using it.

In the fifteen or so years in which the program has been in operation, many millions of dollars in savings have been gained through the polled ideas of ordinary employees. Every person becomes an ideas man or woman, and innovation in methods and products isn't limited to the "idea departments" such as industrial engineering or research.

"Brainstorming" is a technique often used in connection with idea-getting which has produced some amazing results. The term and its application grew out of advertising man Alex Osborn's attempts to improve the creativity of copy writers, and has been adopted wholesale by industry. Charles Clark, when with Ethyl Corporation, has reported amazing success in the use of this stimulating technique which uses the group approach to idea getting.

The procedure is to gather together people with varied experience in a conference room and throw out a problem to them. The major rules are that no negative reactions are allowed. Every idea, no matter how wild, that might solve the problem is sought. Since one idea suggests another, this association of minds often pulls out unique ideas that might have been discarded before evaluation under ordinary circumstances.

With all of the ideas out and listed, a smaller group then takes the record of the brainstorming and evaluates each fully for any possible applications. This freeing of the imagination has the effect of eliminating the barriers to ideas which grow out of resentment of subordinates' ideas by supervisors; of the fellow who says "we tried that before" or the fellow who suggests that "our business is different." Moreover, people report it to be stimulating and often results in a change in attitude of the hard-shelled individuals toward reception of new ideas once presented.

Ultimately however, such ideas must be evaluated from the practical viewpoint of their value and practicality. This ordinarily falls to a few people who have the broad picture of the needs and procedures of the firm, and can fit new ideas into operations.

> Continental Can Company found some profitable savings through brainstorming the question of how to use the angle irons which came to guard corners of tin plate from the mill. Previously these had been scrapped and sold for a fraction of their value. Over 50 usable ideas for commercially producable products or money-saving uses came out of the scrap iron piece.

The use of any ideas from employees however will only occur when the relationship between the manager and his subordinates is one that is satisfactory to both. If the man feels that his opinions are wanted—or even sought after—they'll be forthcoming. This implies a condition that has been described as democratic leadership.

How Democratic Leadership Works

Using such a term as democratic leadership can bring about some confusion in the minds of people who have associated the terms with political democracy, the mechanics of party politics, and elections. As it's used in industry, however, the mechanics are different. The real justification for the term democratic means the underlying philosophy of political and industrial government, rather than the mechanics by which each is applied. Obviously these procedures are different ones for the two different circumstances.

Perhaps a more accurate way of describing democratic leadership in management is to apply the term *responsiveness.* Where the manager is not at all responsive, and simply makes his decisions and announces them for others to execute there is certainly no democratic leadership. The degrees of responsiveness to the wishes, needs, desires, and aspirations of his followers is the true measure of how democratic his leadership is.

Friendliness of his employees may have little or nothing to do with responsiveness to their needs. Employees may hold the most friendly feelings toward an autocrat who has provided them with security. Even a dictator is aware of the need for avoiding hostility in the ranks of those he rules, and simply meeting this standard implies no great virtue as a democratic leader to the manager who simply accomplishes this. Since every leader must achieve at least this much to survive, there's little merit in claiming such an accomplishment.

Responsiveness implies a mutual regard, and becomes important to the manager who wants to make things happen in the modern company because he will thus make available to himself and the organization he leads the pooled talents of his subordinates. This pooled talent can be voted positively or negatively as the group decides, and when thrown into the struggle favorably provides a distinct advantage to the leader who elicits it.

The minimum requirement of responsiveness is a willingness to change a decision if he detects that the prevailing opinion is such that it is not acceptable to the majority of people, unless overpowering considerations of urgency require that it be done. Perhaps the dividing line between democratic management and other kinds is where the supervisor presents problems rather than his own solution.

> There's a law of administration which I'd suggest holds true in almost every situation. That is, if the boss presents his solution first, and asks opinions of his solution, he'll get a vote of approval almost every time.

Responsiveness and democratic management means that the boss asks for other's solutions to a problem which affects the people whose opinion he solicits, and listens to their suggestions before announcing his own.

As he gets the ideas of his subordinates the manager widens his ambit of information upon which he can make the decision.

> One large company holds pre-bargaining sessions with their supervisors before going into contract negotiations with their union. Each is asked to comment upon possible union demands, and to comment upon the present union contract as to workability. These comments are taken into consideration when bargaining gets under way.

Still even more responsive and perhaps an untypical example for that reason is the form of leadership which permits the group to make its own decisions. Employee recreation committees often function within the framework of a budget allocated by management. The only provision is that the committee must fairly represent the employees' interests in recreation, and spend no more than the money allocated or chargeable for specific events. Joint employee committees on safety, on housekeeping, and the administration of certain employee-oriented functions such as the credit union, the welfare fund and other functions come close to this form of management.

Less frequently applied, but stoutly defended by its advocates are those forms which let employees set their own standards of work. Professor Bavelas of MIT has conducted numerous research projects upon the use of employee participation in decision making, and almost unanimously the results have been favorable from a management viewpoint.

The important variable in such management methods isn't in its techniques however, but in the philosophy which underlies it. Presumption that employees are responsible and mature and will arrive at responsible decisions if entrusted with the power to do so isn't one of gadgets and methods. It's a function of the basic attitude of people.

Two pressing reasons indicate that newer techniques are needed which press further in the direction of more democracy in management.

1. Our nation is democratic, and the needs for extending this democracy into the places where people work are quite pertinent. Many serious people of conservative bent are asking if we can keep alive the democratic instincts and abilities of citizens to make free and intelligent choices if they lack opportunity in the place they spend most of their waking, creative hours—their jobs.

2. There is a preponderance of evidence which shows that responsiveness to the needs of people and democratic management is the only feasible way of obtaining the benefit of the pooled brainpower of the employees of a firm for innovation. The value of the asset which lies in the worker is immense, and tapping this is worth the efforts of the best management knowledge we can muster.

7

Rigid Managers—
Making Them More Flexible

"It is well for the world that in most of us, by the age of thirty, the character has set like plaster, and will never soften again."

——WILLIAM JAMES

One of the toughest problems for the top manager is dealing with an important member of the management team who is too rigid.

This rigid man won't see anybody's viewpoint but his own, and often resents any suggestion that he should change. Much has been written and said about the fellow who resists change because of habit or insecurity, and longs for the good old days. There's another type of rigid man in managment, however, who's rigid for different reasons. He's inflexible because he's overly oriented to his own department or specialty.

Within his specialty, such as accounting, engineering, sales, or manufacturing, he may actually be progressive. His problem—and management's problem—is that he can't see anything but his own special division as having any real importance in the business. This makes him not only difficult to do business with, but impossible to promote.

For his own, and the company's good, management needs to do something to break down his rigidity. Six ways of doing this have proved helpful when properly used:

- Job rotation.
- Coaching and counseling.
- Civic and community activities.
- Management courses.
- Psychological counseling.
- Surrounding him.

Rigid people weren't born that way. To some extent, the specialized nature of modern jobs forces people to adopt habit patterns that become rigid. Like automobile drivers who are perfect gentlemen when afoot but turn into raging maniacs at the wheel, the rigid men are often affable fellows outside the job.

Although the psychologists warn us against stereotyping everyone we meet, it's not too dangerous and is sometimes helpful to have some general guides to recognizing the rigid men in management. In most companies they fall into five major types.

1. The manufacturing type.
2. The engineering type.
3. The sales type.
4. The accounting-financial type.
5. The staff type.

Not everyone in these areas is the rigid type, of course, but it is easy to recognize those who are. It is even easy to overemphasize rigid behavior in the other fellow.

Everyone in manufacturing knows how rigid the controller is; and the sales people know how rigid manufacturing people can be.

It's tougher to face up to your own rigidity. Behaving in a certain way consistently is often a logical response to the situation in which a smart man finds himself in the company. Most successful managers start out in some specialty and prove their mettle in it before being given a chance at more general management jobs. It's during this early apprenticeship that the rigidities creep in and sometimes never go away.

If you sometimes wonder if you may be getting too set in your ways, you might run a quiet check on yourself. If one of the following descriptions seems to fit you, you may want to consider ways, with or without company help, of breaking out of the pattern.

The Rigid Manufacturing Boss

You're rigid in this job if you have a deep conviction that you are the only real he-man in the company; a hairy-chested, two-fisted, masculine type who makes things happen. Presses bang, machines clatter, and men sweat at your bidding. Because of you the stuff goes out the back door, and all's right with the world because you are manly and tough.

Naturally, everyone not in manufacturing is a little bit befuddled. They don't get action. They fiddle around with nice words and pieces of paper.

You hit the ball, get action, crash through to the goal. Occasionally you discover you are correcting the same things over and over again, but that's because of some incompetent people the personnel department sent you. What's needed is harder drive, more demand for results; take no excuses, cut through delay. Your worst insult is to call somebody "impractical." *You're rigid if you can only think in terms of action.*

The Rigid Engineer

You're the possessor of a wonderful instrument called the engineering mind which has a monopoly on logic. You combine the knowledge of the scientist, the mathematician, chemist or physicist with the ability to turn this logic into beautiful and practical objects. This engineering mind sees every subject more clearly, and defines the essence more succinctly than any one who doesn't possess it. You can't stand anything but facts . . . you are made ill by people who play politics, talk glibly, verbalize too freely, turning the business into a wind tunnel of hot air. Things and facts can be counted on. People and verbal abstractions can't, so it's best to go it by yourself, then you can be sure it's done right. You are under-rated by your employer (who is living off your brain), by your wife, and by society generally. *You're rigid if you stress things and ignore people.*

The Rigid Salesman

People don't really understand you. They think you are a huckster, an extrovert, back-slapper. Yours is really a creative job which is based upon the solid human instinct of wanting money.

You know that the dollar is the lubricant that makes the wheels turn. Being a hot salesman makes you free of discipline and company rules. Salesmanship is the basis of our civilization. Under this plan everyone is either a customer or a salesman. If you are the customer, you can rough up people such as waiters, other salesmen, hotel managers, and taxi drivers and patch their wounds with a buck, because anybody will jump for a price. Buyers are entitled to treat you the same way, of course. Things will always be better than they are now, and pep, drive, and the discipline of the dollar are the keys to success, which is what everyone really wants. You'd crawl a mile over broken bottles to get a fat order. *You're rigid if you see satisfaction only in money.*

The Rigid Cost Accountant

Every day you lay out on sheets of paper the essence of the business, and control it by changing figures in the columns. You sit at the eye of the storm, the nerve center of the company, and watch for signs that mean the ship is about to founder. You issue memos or whisper words to the captain and he issues the commands you have suggested which save the ship. The others only think they are the key men with their wild rushing and frantic activity. You are the hourly savior of the business; you police trickling little losses that would turn into torrents if you weren't there. As the master scorekeeper and conservator you must be cold, passionless, without emotion. You can't afford to be loved because you might let a little leak turn into a big drain if you ruled by your emotions. Yours is a higher responsibility, and your manner and dress should reflect this weighty burden. Your pleasures are simple as with all men whose every decision is a weighty one. *You're rigid if you see business only as figures.*

The Rigid Staff Type

You don't make anything, or sell it, but you are master of something which is vitally more necessary to the preservation of the business—it's called a procedure. A procedure implements a sacrosanct guide called a policy, which is never subject to question. Life in the office is to you one of great frustration in which people who don't follow procedures cause you endless work and trouble. You tell them about procedures but they persist in doing things in their own foolish, individual way.

You are pressed by numerous competing forces, the hostility of line people, the demands of top management to which you have no recourse, and the frustration of never really completing a task because people in the line ignore procedures. The solution, you know, will come when you can devise more procedures which will prevent further lapses from policies and procedures not now being followed. *You're rigid if you think a business is no more than a set of procedures.*

Corrective Action

To break people of rigidities is a job of enlarging people. They've got to become generalists instead of specialists.

This provides us with the key to breaking people out of the rigidities which they build into their behavior on certain jobs.

1. *Job rotation.* One way of breaking a man out of a rigid attitude is to let him see the other fellow's viewpoint first-hand by putting him in that fellow's position. The manufacturing man who faces adamant customers as a salesman gets a good look at what marketing really means. The controller who spends some time in the plant finds out why certain

extraordinary expenses are often required. The staff man who came to the position from a line job is often a better man than the fellow who has held nothing but a home office job. The salesman who does a tour of duty in manufacturing learns some of the problems of making the orders he has been bringing in for rush delivery. The engineer who follows through his design to manufacture goes back to the drawing board as a better engineer.

2. *Coaching and counseling.* Because job rotation is sometimes impossible and often too expensive, a more practical method of breaking people out of their mold is to hold regular coaching sessions with them. These are talks on "How'm I doing?" between the boss and his subordinate which deal with some of the subordinate's acts and behavior which indicate rigidity and lack of appreciation for other departments' problems.

Such coaching can be on a planned and formal basis, and is best supplemented by frequent, informal chats on a day-to-day basis. If the boss is a generalist himself his warmth and humanity may shine through and be imitated.

3. *Civic and community activities.* Sending executives out to work on community activities is an excellent way of giving them some broadening, and seeing that the formula for success they have adopted on the job isn't the only way things get done in the world. The manufacturing man who heads up a volunteer campaign for funds shortly discovers that persuasion and diplomacy are arts which have their place, too. He will come back a bigger and better man for it. Letting executives serve on boards of community associations is a good way of accomplishing the same goal.

4. *Management courses and seminars.* Sending people away to general management courses and seminars is a widely tried and proven way of helping a rigid man see himself in his true light. Placed in a strange situation where everybody is a big wheel like himself, he may discover that the tried and true attitudes he has used are not necessarily the only ones or even the best ones. Where such courses entail free-wheeling discussion he may discover that he has to examine his own attitudes and methods of handling problems if he is to convince others. This is good for creating flexibility.

5. *Psychological counseling.* Occasionally a top man just doesn't respond to any of these treatments and may be rigid because of some deep-seated attitudes dating back to childhood. It's wisest at this point to try to get professional assistance. If the company has a staff psychologist, the prob-

lem might be explained to him, and a series of meetings for counseling arranged.

The principal purpose here is to have the psychologist help the executive to see several basic facts:

- He has certain attitudes affecting his job performance which are damaging his future and are affecting company operations.
- That only he can make the necessary changes in his attitude which will result in more human behavior.

The psychologist often is able to give the man greater insight into his own behavior, and help him to program a change in his work behavior.

6. *Surround him.* Some companies and certain executives won't stand still for psychological counseling for a variety of reasons.

Under these circumstances many companies organize around the man so that his special skills and abilities can be used effectively, while his disruptive habits are ameliorated by people who act as his assistants or colleagues.

In one large company, for example, a noted scientist in top management was constantly disrupting the operations of the lab through his arrogance and inflexibility.

Top management assigned an administrative assistant to handle his housekeeping chores, and to deal with customers, accountants, manufacturing people, and others. Not only did the assistant learn a lot, but the man himself was relieved to perform his specialty.

The top manufacturing man who is inflexible may require bolstering with clerks, administrative assistants, or understudies who protect the organization from the disruptions growing out of his inflexibility.

In an age when the specialist is more and more in demand, we find more and more companies taking conscious steps to offset some of the bad effects of specialist behavior that becomes overspecialized. The need isn't to eliminate specialization, but to get the specialists who have become rigid to bend to the needs of the whole enterprise.

8

How to Change Poor
Work Habits to Good

"Those who think must govern those who toil."

—OLIVER GOLDSMITH

No single tool or technique of scientific management gives a company more competitive advantage than a staff of people whose work habits are good.

Where do employees get their work habits, and how can they be improved?

A work habit is built up from four basic sources:

1. The early training, including schools and family, which the employee brought with him.

2. His own experience in the company, especially the earliest experience. Many work habits are set the first day on the job, and unless corrected never substantially change.

3. The group with which the employee is located. If he's with a hardworking bunch he'll put out more to keep up with them; if he's with a more casual team he'll match his pace to theirs, otherwise they won't accept him.

4. The boss. Responsibility for work habits can be laid almost fully in his lap, since he is in a position to make amends for the other three causes through constructive action.

Basically there are eight principal ways in which the boss can change work habits of an employee. Sometimes a single one will do the trick. In more persistent cases it will take a combination of all eight. The formula must be tailored to individual circumstances. While psychologists can explain many intricate motivation and apititude factors, it's more practical for the working manager to approach the subject from the viewpoint of work habits than to plunge too deeply into the employee's libido and how he reacted to his babysitter. It is primarily job performance that interests the manager. If the employee lapses into lazy habits outside the job, that shouldn't be of too much concern.

Admittedly this is a rule-of-thumb method, but it gets at the main point and is relatively uncomplicated. The eight ways in which work habits can be improved include:

- Watch the work pattern of employees.
- Replace the bad habit with a good one.
- Start the new employee right.
- Show the employee a reason for changing.
- Try the job yourself.
- Set a good example.
- Work through the informal organization.
- Get participation.

Let's see how each of these steps works in practice:

Watch the Work Pattern

Both simple and complicated jobs will settle into repetitive patterns of work activity. This pattern may be of the employee's own devising, or it may be taught. Once acquired it will be adhered to. This pattern is characteristic of complex jobs as well as simple, routine ones, except that the pattern may be more extended in scope and is often called a procedure.

These work patterns are not rationally evaluated. In the day-to-day routine of the job a person will follow the repetitive cycle in a more or less unthinking manner. This isn't necessarily undesirable. Without such patterns, our lives would consist of a series of deliberations and decisions about such things as walking, chewing, writing, and other routine things. The rub comes when we build into our routines a lot of time-consuming activities that mean we don't get done the things we would like to get done. We build in trips to the water-cooler, to the stock room, social chats with fellow workers simply because we haven't formed the habit of bearing down on the top priority jobs ahead.

The man with the poor work habits spends as much energy as the hard worker, but fritters and putters around with trivia. Observing the pattern to improve work habits means watching for this shuffling and duplication.

Replace a Bad Habit with a Good One

The primary tool in improving work habits is substitution. After getting some idea of the major patterns and finding where the time-robbing portions lie, replace them with something productive. This means breaking the cycle that adds up to undesirable parts. In some cases this can be done by a physical re-arrangement of the work place at the time the change is introduced. Habits tend to be associated with physical activity. It's also an axiom that the worker will more readily accept the new method if he's allowed to participate in the change which affects him.

In one instance a manager was able to combine a frank chat with his worst offender in work habits with a change in desk location. By breaking his routine of work-a-little followed by head-for-the-water-cooler and other similar dilatory tactics he was able to show the man that the major block to his effectiveness and personal advancement was that he was in a rut. The change of scene, coupled with some candid talk, did the trick.

In another case, replacing a bad habit with a good one took the form of pitching a man with some sloppy work habits a tough chore first thing in the morning. Where he previously had started off the day with fumbling, foot-shuffling and floundering that sometimes lasted all day, he now found that he was required to pull together some important information from overnight quickly and accurately and have it on the boss's desk within twenty minutes of starting time. This momentum began to carry on into the rest of the day.

Start the New Employee Right

Many a work habit of a decade's standing began with the first morning the man began on the job. A new employee will be most eager to succeed, and will accept the work cycle presented to him by the first instructor or coach he encounters. This means that, before the cycle becomes habitual, it should be studied for idle and observation time and the blanks filled up. With good training, proper method and procedures will be taught the first time the man encounters the job. The induction step can't be entrusted to people whose work habits are poor.

More than one manager has been heard to say that he can't waste time doing a full-scale training job for the new man. Pressed for details, it often turns out that the reason he hasn't time for training new employees is because he's patching up the faulty training of old ones who, like the present recruits, couldn't be adequately inducted because of the pressures of time.

Show a Reason for Better Habits

Changing work habits with any degree of permanence requires some motivation. In some instances profit-sharing, incentive, or bonus plans already exist and are a ready-made reason for the employee to work more effectively. If it can be demonstrated that the new work pattern will benefit the man, he will tend to hang onto it.

Where no monetary incentive exists, it often helps to show him that the new method is really less fatiguing, less dangerous, or eliminates some difficulty which he has been experiencing. In some cases opportunity to advance is good motivation. Where these elements are lacking, it may be necessary to stress benefits to the company.

In these instances it can be pointed out that by working more effectively he actually increases his security and opportunity in his job, since he improves the company's competitive position.

In a few instances where a youngster without prior work experience or an employee who has been spoiled by poor supervision is involved, more strict action is demanded. After all explanation and selling is complete, it becomes necessary to inform the employee that he must change or disciplinary action will follow. It's often advisable in such cases to make the disciplinary procedure a three-step one, letting the employee know each step from the beginning.

1. Inform the employee his work habits are not up to company standards; show him evidence and suggest some specific steps to improve them.

2. If the employee ignores or refuses to follow the suggested steps he should then be warned that he will be disciplined. It's better to be specific than to generalize.

3. Continued lapses from better habits should result in temporary layoff, or possibly discharge. In any event, don't transfer him to another department within the company unless he shows some evidence of physical or mental inability to do the job the way you want it done. Transfers have no magic power of improving work habits, and are only justified when they bring about a better fit between man and job.

Try the Job Yourself

In some cases it's a sound idea to take a stab at doing the job yourself to find out if the employee actually has good work habits but is performing at what seems to be low output because of things in the job which aren't apparent to the naked eye. Many an experienced employee is working at peak performance but makes it look simple to outsiders. He may have vastly greater efficiency than you imagined. This is often true of the best employees. Before sailing into the person who seems to be relaxed and comfortable on his job you'd better quietly take his place for a little while. It's not always easy to judge how hard a task is from observation.

Set a Good Example

Not long ago I walked through a medical supply plant with a company executive. Several yards away he spotted a small piece of debris on the floor. Breaking off our conversation he walked over and picked up the scrap and put it in his pocket.

"I wouldn't think of letting that piece lie there," he said, "not after all the pressure I put on people to maintain cleanliness and good housekeeping in the plant."

This manager knew that, unless he demonstrated habits of good housekeeping, he probably couldn't expect others to have them either, no matter how loudly he ordered them.

The work habits of the boss have a way of transmitting themselves to the entire organization.

Tie this together with a genuine interest in how well people are performing on their jobs, and periodic talks to let them know how they can improve, and you are on the way to better work habits in the organization.

Use the Informal Organization

One of the most influential factors in shaping work habits is the work group to which a worker is assigned. All workers join informal groups based upon occupational groupings or any one of a dozen or more sentimental or emotional ties such as sex, age, school attended, occupational groups, physical surroundings of work and so forth.

The important thing for the manager is knowledge that these cliques control output of their members, and exercise controls though exclusion and ostracism of people who don't stay in line. A good worker may be soldiering because he doesn't want to be on the outs with his fellow workers. The key to working through informal groups in the work force is the first-line supervisor who is in a position to belong to both management and the clique.

With such leadership in first-line positions, the work habits of individuals will be policed by the group. Without group support of company standards of performance there is little hope of forcing individuals to swim upstream against their fellow workers.

Get Participation

One of the surest ways of getting better work habits and making them stick is to get the wholehearted co-operation of the worker through asking his help and support in improving his own skill and habits. As the expert on his job he can offer more concrete suggestions than anybody.

Once he is involved in changing the pattern it stands a better chance of getting changed for good than if a hundred experts study it and tell him what he should be doing.

Since changed attitudes are vital in changing work habits, participation is another way of saying we get the worker involved in seeing the importance of doing a better job.

In one eastern plant where hand operation on an assembly line was the limitation on output, management let the girls set the speed of the conveyor which carried their work to them. The girls not only exceeded records previously set, but produced so much they caused a problem in the packing station which followed. Asking people to set their own pace doesn't mean they will set it too low. Convinced that mangagement is genuinely interested in them and their views, they will set it higher than might have been anticipated.

Work habits can only be changed by leadership. Experience shows that today toughness alone won't do it.

9

Managing Cliques in the Organization

"No more fiendish punishment could be devised, were such a thing physically possible, than that one should be turned loose in a society and remain absolutely unnoticed by all the members there-of."

—WILLIAM JAMES

The management of cliques is a rapidly growing field for executive action. Already many companies have given up formal organization charting in favor of more sophisticated analysis.

The rewards are obvious: More cooperative people, more productive workers, easier installation of improvements by engineers and accountants, less conflict and confusion rising to the top, greater unity of effort.

Such social scientists as Dr. Chris Argyris of Yale have studied and written extensively on the subject of cliques. Some describe the possibility of better management of informal organizations as the next great breakthrough in management theory and practice. These scientists declare that the dual goals of the clique in business—desire for security and for participation in the decisions which affect them—are finding their way into organization planning in many firms. No mere academic exercise, the management of the clique is for high stakes.

For one thing, cost reduction programs have often pointed up the fact that the people at the top of the organization can't seem to maintain touch with the people at the bottom, no matter how loudly they shout or how keenly they listen. Probes to find the reason have indicated that the clique is a block to real communication.

For another thing, information about policies, procedures, rules and regulations doesn't come out at one end in the form of behavior the boss intended when he put it in at the other. Systems which are completely logical just don't work the way they were designed to work. Industrial engineers seem to find new heights of employee and clique ingenuity in undermining incentives and methods improvement.

Still another management problem which seems to center around the clique organization is the failure of specialist groups to coordinate, mainly because they become special interest groups which don't communicate. In many engineering and research labs, for example, the multiplication of technical jargon by the cliques has become almost comparable to a tower of Babel.

Multiplied throughout the company, it's more than the electrical engineers not pulling in harness with the mechanicals; it's the accounting clique battling the sales clique, the quality clique scrimmaging the production crowd, the union bunch fighting everybody, the office fighting the shop, the old-timers fighting the young college Turks, and the company losing in every case.

Finally, the cliques are the building blocks of that much criticized figure, the organization man. The clique makes its members conformists who suppress their individuality in order to retain membership and popularity with the informal group with which they work. To the extent that the clique places no premium upon individual effort or creativity, the skills of imitation and cooperation become paramount.

As the full dimension of the clique's influence becomes more apparent, many of the methods for handling human relations and communications problems become increasingly inadequate, overmatched by the problems they are expected to solve.

In format the clique appears as a small group; the graduates of a particular school, practitioners of a special occupation, or a few people bound together by ties of sentiment, common interests, or like social ties.

The clique is a spontaneous, informal, natural cultural formation inside the organization. It controls its members through social pressures and can act either favorably or unfavorably insofar as the company is concerned.

Since management can neither order the clique out of existence nor circumvent it by industrial engineering or directives, the logical course is to prevail on the group to act in the firm's interest.

A number of steps can lead toward this result. Summarized, these include:

- Recognize that cliques exist.
- Train managers to deal with them.

- Catalog the major segments of the clique organization.
- Study operating techniques of cliques.
- Work through informal leaders.
- Plan facilities so they will establish social status.

Recognize Cliques Exist

Cliques exist in every human organization, including the family, the church, unions, the government, as well as business firms. No master plan or sinister conspiracy is needed to start one—only a few people having common interests, fear of the boss, or pride of achievement. Many large and imposing clubs have grown out of a clique founded on the habits, likes, dislikes, sentiments, interests and endowments of a group of individuals.

Management which, on hearing that cliques exist, reacts with an emotional outburst aimed at wiping them out or with a denial that they have infiltrated the company is merely putting obstacles in the way of steps which might lead to a more sophisticated treatment of the subject.

Acceptance of cliques as going concerns, and an effort to understand their nature and scope, will pay dividends in the adoption of policies and practices designed to enlist them into channels of help and increased productivity.

Train Managers

One of the basic steps in getting a grasp on the clique situation must include some basic training of management in group relations and the specifics of informal organization. Human relations training in the past has often been oriented toward studies of individual behavior without attention to the group processes.

Although it's obvious that the group consists of individuals, mere understanding of individual motivation without some practical knowledge of how the clique modifies this behavior is only half the story.

Mary Jones may want to produce more work in the typing pool; but she has learned that if she is too productive she won't be invited to the little luncheon and gossip dates which also are important to her. With cliques in mind we still study the individual; but we pay more attention to how Mary meets her individual needs through group approval.

John Jones, engineer, may be more interested in what the boys down at the engineering society think of him than what his boss thinks, or even of what he thinks of himself.

Putting this basic importance of the group across to the supervisor, the manager, the technician and the staff man is a key step in managing the informal organization.

Catalog Clique Segments

With a management and staff aware of the importance and nature of cliques, a company can catalog the major cliques and learn how they react to one another and to the company. This is best done by the people who are actually on the spot as managers, engineers, and staff people. The foreman of Department 10, for example, will know his people as individuals, and can easily plot out the major cliques in his department.

He knows that the mechanics are one clique, the old-timers another, the operators of certain sections a third, and so on. He can further tell how they get along, who is considered highest on the social scale of the shop, who likes whom.

Top management can usually spot the major clique divisions.

In one chemical company, for example, the major clique consists of graduate chemists who will move up the line in management. Generally the four major subdivisions of cliques will include:

- Top management—the boys on mahogany row.
- Supervisors—the white-collar bosses in the shop.
- Technicians—accountants, engineers, and others whose work is primarily concerned with improving other people's effectiveness.
- Workers—the clerks, typists, machine operators, laborers, salesmen.

Within each of these major subdivisions are cliques. Even in top brass there will be cliques. The girls in the secretarial pool from a particular school may be a worker clique, the engineers in the sales force, or the Harvard Business School men in executive row.

In looking for cliques, the key seems to be to identify common ties which people might have. These ties can be affection, pride, insecurity, hatred, or simple gregariousness. The resulting cliques will have similar forms. Usually they are about as strong as the emotion which caused the members to drift together into a clique in the first place. Sometimes direct questioning will elicit accurate answers about cliques.

People are especially aware of cliques above them in social status, or to which they aspire. They often deny the existence of their own, not because they want to hide its existence, but simply because they don't recognize it as one.

Study Clique Operating Techniques

The most important operating technique from a business viewpoint is the clique's ability to control its members' actions, especially their productivity, creativity and cooperativeness. A worker, who does more work than the clique has arbitrarily decided is a safe or decent amount, risks ostracism. This control system can work to restrict output or upset the most soundly planned incentive system. It can also carry through to fabulous success any management plan which fits in with the special goals the clique has set. It resists change with enormous effectiveness.

The weapons of control most often used are exclusion from social contact, failure to include in luncheon groups, small talk or help on the job.

The clique rations congeniality and warmth, and sometimes extends outside the plant into the community. Unless the offender has some hope of being included in a different and better clique, there is little chance of his swimming upstream against his own clique.

The supervisor who can identify the cliques and their control systems can go further and seek out the basis of clique standards of control.

The best leaders get the clique pulling for them. In fact, they become informal leaders of the clique as well as the formal leaders assigned by management. The most effective and productive teams are cliques that have aligned their own goals with those of the administration.

In such cases, the full power and ability of the group will be brought to bear, and the results will be unsurpassed anywhere.

Assigning good workers to a hostile clique or one with low standards can only result in spoiling the worker. On the other hand, putting a loafer with a hard-working group can often boost his performance up to the group standard through clique controls.

One key indicator of group operating methods is a special language. Often this is simply a new use of plain English. In other cases it involves development of special jargon, such as "gandy dancer" on the railroads. Often these words are functional words commonly used in the day-to-day technical aspects of the job. In others, they are simply profanity. Occasionally, they are inside jokes, or hints, and innuendoes.

The manager who is sensitive and observant will find that these things are open signs which a keen observer can interpret. With such indications of group sentiment, the manager can take steps to avert bad results, and encourage favorable ones, if he can interpret these signs as evidence of the modus operandi of the clique. In some cases, he may be required to proceed regardless of group sentiment, but with forewarning of resistance.

In other cases, he can try a different approach, or even defer his action with a view to winning clique support for his plan.

Working Through Informal Leaders

Every informal organization has its informal leaders. These leaders are not appointed by management, or selected by plebiscite, and have no guaranteed tenure. They are the individuals who seem best to articulate the emotional state of the group, and are most sensitive to its sentiments. Once established they are entitled to lead the group in particular situations, policing backsliders, and setting an example for the rest.

It is here that the greatest opportunity exists for working through the clique. If the assigned leader, foreman, office manager, or executive can earn the support of the clique, he will become its leader, even though he has a singular role in the group and serves management first.

If he speaks the language of the clique, he holds a key to moving the group toward standards which are satisfactory to the company and at the same time pleasing to the clique.

By controlling the communication system, he exercises special powers over group behavior. In practice, he can hold onto his informal leadership only so long as the group identifies him as being one of them. Once excluded because he has threatened the group's solidarity or made it feel inadequate, he will lose this control.

The group operates in such a way that a foreman may also be accepted by a worker clique, because cliques are loose groupings and a single individual may belong to several of them, even those with opposing interests—without such affiliations seeming inconsistent.

A person who is in good standing in several cliques is in a position to bring about teamwork, cooperation, and unity of effort.

The evidence seems to point to the organization man as the best manager for getting the clique to pull toward company goals. The nonconformist who wears a beard and Bermuda shorts to work can be productive only so long as the clique accepts this as normal behavior and him as one of the group. Tossed out of membership by the clique, the loner is likely to become so ineffective that he will be discharged for inefficiency, not merely because he fell out of step with the group.

Managers normally find that they need the cooperation of three or more cliques in order to function with any success.

They are obliged to get cooperation the informal organization way. Informal leadership as a method of managing then becomes skill in joining several cliques without seeming to be inconsistent to any of them. From inside, a leader can sway the group toward the company goals.

Planning Facilities

The physical facilities of the plant or office are important in managing the clique organization. Every desk, every chair, every office, telephone, rug, and tool used in the technical performance of work has a veneer of social significance in addition to its functional usage.

These serve to establish the social status of the persons to whom they are assigned. So do inequities in the assignment of office space, in tools and in differences in pay.

Being founded on sentiment, the clique cannot rise above the somewhat petty considerations of small differences in working conditions. It will buzz loudly at changes in desks, work layout, conveniences, and facilities which the social scientists call status symbols. Complaints are not based on actual physical comfort or discomfort, but on the social effects of change on the group.

In one case, a group of draftsmen in a New Jersey company stopped work because new air conditioners were installed in their department. Baffled by this reaction, the chief engineer spent several hours chatting with a delegation, explaining how the pieces were chosen, who selected them, and explaining "why the draftsmen weren't consulted."

Consulting key cliques may be an important consideration in managing the clique; the careful detailed planning of facilities. Often it means that key cliques must be involved in this planning; or at best, the managers of the respective departments must be consulted on the possible ramifications of such change.

10

Coaching a Winning Management Team

"I'd define coaching as the job of getting men to play up to the best of their natural endowments."

—FRITZ CRISLER

Any youngster who's ever followed the circus knows that one of the miracles of the business is the setting up and taking down of the show. The job most commonly seen by the public is that of driving tent stakes, in which three men armed with sledges, all drive the same stake into the ground with blows struck in quick succession. For the roustabout who let his hammer strike atop another, or permitted his own to be so slow in pulling away that it was struck by the next would be laughed from the gang. In stringing the lines, raising the canvas, breaking up the side show, or linking the caravan into a mobile unit the roustabouts work with teamwork which is a circus tradition. However this system of teamwork was originated—some say by P. T. Barnum—the effect of early coaching has been felt on circuses ever since. The ultimate effect of good coaching is one of effective teamwork in business as well.

Assuming a managerial position where such coordination and teamwork doesn't exist in an industrial organization presents one of the great challenges of the management job. The major reason for this is that the fruits of good coaching are apt to last longer than any single effect which a manager can bring about in an organization.

One of the finest teams I've seen in the work place was on the assembly line for the manufacture of insecticide cans of the American Can Company in New Jersey. An automatic line, small squares of tin were placed in at the head of the line (the bodymaker) and the finished cans finally disappeared through a hole in the floor at the other end without any halting. In successive stages the can was flanged, the bottom seamed on, the top seamed on, a nozzle placed on the top, soldered tight, and the can tested for leaks in a giant air wheel. Operators fed materials and parts into machines at various stages along the line, but the cans flowed through and paced the operators at thousands every hour. On the surface it would seem that no opportunity existed for teamwork. Every person had his job of filling the feed of his machine and not much more. Yet the operators on these lines played extra roles. These occurred when a breakdown, or jam, occurred in one of the machines. Immediately a whistled signal set machine operators into motion. A jam on the second machine, for example, brought the operator of the first machine around to the end of his machine where he stacked the off-coming cans on a bench until the jam was removed by the second operator. Once the machine was going the two operators used the spare seconds available while the line was running to feed the bank of stacked-off cans into the line. In a few minutes they patched up the shortage which might have occurred due to the jam-up. Along the length of the line this double-teaming to help one another maintain a steady flow of cans all through the day was an ordinary condition of team work.

The difference which teamwork made in this crew was made apparent each time a new and untried man entered the department to work, or where an entire new crew was put on, such as a new second shift. In every such case the person did his job exactly as the job description specified. Their attitude was good, and they desired to cooperate. Yet, without coaching and the resultant teamwork they never produced as much. In short, coaching is the margin of the superior over the ordinary which can be obtained in a situation.

Building efficiency through coaching new crews, or coaching experienced people in better team play in this case, wasn't a simple thing that could be accomplished in a week or two.

Was it worth the effort? Most definitely.

An air of competence hung over the "top crew" as they referred to themselves. Their record of production and effectiveness was infectious and new individuals who joined the crew were helped and given tips on coming up to the group standards quite rapidly.

For work groups in office, staff, and professional fields it would seem that there are some distinct things that a manager does to achieve teamwork.

1. *Assignment.* He spends some time in carefully picking, or checking the assignments of, the individuals who will play on the team or work

in the group. This is more than selection for general abilities. It consists of matching the man to the individual job he'll do, and to the team with which he'll have to work.

2. *Teach basics first.* In assigning the man to the job, or sharpening his individual skill, he slowly and patiently goes through all of the *basic* requirements of the job, one step at a time until he's sure they have them. This stress on fundamentals continues with every employee until each man's confidence and adeptness are solidly built into his performance.

3. *Condition the group.* He conditions the group to accept the new man. If it's an already existing group he spends some time getting to know each member of the group and smoothing out frictions and confusion between the individual members. He points out ways in which helping one another makes things easier for all. He indicates his approval of team play, and his disappointment at selfishness and obstreperousness.

4. *Show interest.* The coach who sits in the stand and reads the newspaper or listens to another game isn't going to generate much support from his team. If it's a productive, competent team they want the coach observing, saying a good word, giving them tips on new jobs coming up and asking them how things are going.

5. *Make changes carefully.* A smoothly functioning work team is often governed best by the rule of "hands off." Changes of a minor nature for specific individuals involve some individual coaching and instruction. These are generally quite acceptable. Drastic changes in the entire format —presumably the same team will exist and must execute them—are best approached cautiously and with the acceptance of the group achieved through discussion and participation.

Picking and Training Good Players

For the action-getting manager his coaching plan begins with a hard look at each person on the team. Does he have the capacity to do the job? Is there a better way of assigning him? Is he learning and growing? Does he fit into the group with which he's working?

> A staff department of a large corporation had a vacancy for a top flight engineer who had lots of operating experience. After some careful screening—or so they thought—a twenty year man from a plant manager's position in the field was transferred into the staff department. Within a short time it became apparent that he wasn't going to do at all. For one thing he could not write a decent letter or memo. His plant job had not required it, and he had never developed the skill. More than that his relations with others was awkward because of his rough language. With young secretaries

and clerical people who saw themselves as more genteel than his former associates in the mill, his habit of addressing equals with clubbiness and profanity isolated him from the group. Eventually he had to be reassigned to the plant—a much happier man.

Good assignment and selection doesn't always means that every member of the team must be a paragon. In one metal working plant it was customary to take the most troublesome employees, the roughnecks, the mavericks, the rebels and assign them to the foundry. The foreman of the foundry had capitalized on this fact—without necessarily letting management know what he was doing—and greeted every newcomer with:

"What did you do wrong to get assigned here? Every one of us down here in the black gang has been kicked out of the civilized society upstairs. I want you to know that we can show those guys how to put-out . . . you've got to be rough to live down here. If that doesn't suit your taste then get the hell upstairs now."

This reverse motivation worked beautifully. The work output and tolerance for the noise, heat, and back-breaking labor was fantastic. The language was rough, the work brutal, but morale and output unmatched anywhere in the shop. To have picked an overly sensitive or "promising" young man and assigned him there would have ruined both the man and the work team.

Occasionally the very hardships and special difficulties of the working conditions can become a rallying point for a team. Certainly the most effective teams ever built were those of the infantry or marines.

Training people to function effectively with the group is simple job instruction. This will always follow a sound instruction in basics of their individual job. The Job Instruction Training programs of World War II proved wonderfully effective for quickly training persons without experience in factory operations to assume defense jobs in vital industry, and arrive at peak effectiveness within the shortest possible time. This formula went as follows:

1. Prepare the learner (make him want to learn, etc.)
2. Present the operation (patiently show and tell him one step at a time until you're sure he knows)
3. Have the learner try the job, and correct his errors
4. Put him on his own, then follow up to see how he's doing.

Before beginning a training session with a worker the instructor prepared himself to instruct through studying the job he was going to teach; making a job breakdown sheet. On this he listed the key points ("anything which will make or break the job is a key point") and got all his materials and the place for instruction ready before starting to train. These basic steps in training are still sound.

Once the man is on his own it should be crystal clear to him what is expected of him by way of output, quality, housekeeping, safety regulations, maintenance of equipment, and all other details of the job. It's not enough to be able to say, "I told him all those things." One of the basic precepts of job instruction is that "if the learner hasn't learned, then the instructor hasn't taught."

Until the new man has been properly trained and followed up on to insure complete familiarity and acceptance of the basic skills of the job he's assigned to, the extra coaching for the fine points of advanced teamwork should be played down. Constant attention to basics will pay great dividends in the coach's scheme of things.

Occasionally a group session with a demonstration which reviews basics in single areas such as safe working habits, quality control, machine maintenance, or others is required.

> In one personnel department it was a regularly scheduled event to hold brief meetings with all clerks, typists, and file clerks upon the need for confidential handling of personnel records. As a result of this regular check-up instruction the personnel office never became the source of rumors and scuttle-butt involving people's pay, their personal records and other information which would have been harmful to the individual and the company to have allowed free dissemination.

In another company the firm hired a famous designer to re-do all of their packaging designs. As a result the cartons and shippers in which the product was shipped and displayed was highly attractive to potential customers, and caught on for the "impulse buyer" in the store. Yet, too many cartons arrived at the store in dishevelled condition. Sealing tapes were either crooked or loose, and there were coffee rings, rips, dents and dirt on the outside. The plant manager, upon hearing of it, called small group meetings of all the employees and explained how the company had gone into the choice of the new design and solicited their cooperation in making the packages as attractive as possible when they left the shipping dock of the plant. This coaching of the group, followed up by reminders by the supervision on the job from time to time completely licked this troublesome problem.

The point here isn't to suggest how a manager should train machine operators, or packers, or even clerks. The important point is that sound coaching begins with training people in basics of their job, and advancing from there to the fine points, niceties, and professional ramifications. This latter stage may be done either through individual talks with employees, small groups, or in a combination of both.

Ten Rules for Good Coaching

Within the pattern of coaching there are ten basic rules for good management coaching:

1. *Know each man.* The first rule of good coaching is to know each employee as an individual. The more information you can obtain, both personal and professional about the employee, the better use you'll be able to make of his capacity. You'll also be able to do a better job of matching strengths and weaknesses of the respective members of the group to the best advantage of the department.

2. *Know what good performance looks like.* The coach can't generally do an effective job of improving performance by dealing in generalities with individuals. They want to know specifically what they are doing that is good, and what they are doing wrong. They want to know what is expected in every detail of their performance, and hope to receive credit for doing it well. This doesn't imply that the coach must be able to do every job better than the man doing it, but he must know very well what's proper performance and be able to judge it accurately. The manager as a coach sees this *judging performance* as an important part of his job.

3. *Stretch people to capacity.* To get high standards of performance it's necessary to set tough but attainable goals which tax the man, and give him something about which he can take pride for success.

> A young lawyer joined the legal department of a large corporation, and worked under the direction of the patent department head. Immediately he was thrown tremendous loads of research and brief writing, investigations and analysis. He had to learn not only all the law he'd failed to master on patents, but also most of the technical details of the company's products.
> "I thought it was impossible for awhile, and hated the old slavedriver I worked for, but I'll have to admit he made a corporation lawyer out of me in a short while."

4. *Show confidence.* The manager as a coach is probably the most important source of optimism and confidence which his work team can have. Groups have a way of swinging up and down in levels of enthusiasm, and require a stabilizer who remains aloof from the swings of emotional fluctuation. Here's what one advertising man told me:

> We introduced a new line with a direct mail campaign and every day we counted the sales returns from the field. Most of the copy-

writers, artists, and production people in the creative departments were ready to open a vein, things looked so gloomy for awhile. Bill, the promotion manager, never wavered a second, though. He kept telling us that we'd done a great job, and that things would turn upward any time. Sure enough, they did, and we were all vastly relieved. Bill never changed. "I knew they would come out OK," was all he said. Either he's got nerves of steel or he's a terrific actor.

Such confidence and steadiness in leadership is a basic requirement for the coach when the team is under pressure. It's the team that doesn't get rattled which wins over one which falls apart under pressure. Under stress, the manager's coaching job may be simply one of setting an example of confidence, and shoring up the more timorous members of the group.

5. *Taking the long view.* The manager in his coaching role holds the major responsibility for keeping the larger objectives of the organization in sight. Under the stress of daily pressures of getting the goods out the back door, or meeting that deadline, there's always the possibility that the long range plan gets gobbled up reaching for short range objectives. Here's what H. B. Woodman, president of the Interchemical Corporation, has said: "The tyranny of the problems of today too often prevents us from doing the long range planning so essential for our corporate success."

6. *Build flexibility in the group.* Basic to good management coaching is working constantly for flexibility. This means more than simply teaching people more than one job—even though that's important too. It means that plans for the future must be adapted quickly to unanticipated or adverse changes in the circumstances of the business.

This flexibility in people is especially tough to achieve where most of the jobs are held by specialists. This specialization causes a narrowness of viewpoint and unwillingness to bend in some instances which must be overcome through coaching.

7. *Pull diverse specialists into a single team.* The manager as a coach is apart from all of the specialists who make up the working corps of the company. It's his job to point out how the behavior of each specialist must be adapted to fit into the over-all pattern of the company. Here's how Charles Thornton, president of Litton Industries, puts it:

> We think of ourselves as specialists with different backgrounds who, as a team, are capable of relating our collective effort to the reality of both today and tomorrow.

Such pulling together means that the manager who is coaching, to accomplish it, makes certain that each specialist has opportunity to see the other fellow's viewpoint, and to know the requirements imposed by the situation of the whole company.

8. *Rate employees by performance not on personal traits.* The business firm is not a family. Accordingly the coach of a business team should have little concern over the personality of the employees except as it directly affects his or his colleagues' performance. It's actually this *performance* on the job which is the coach's first and most important concern. Using abstract lists of characteristics to rate employee performance is not only beside the point in a business firm, it's almost impossible to coach an employee in how to change these things. Rating such things as "attitudes" or "loyalty" is fruitless without specific reference to other performance results. For example, it's worthless for the coach to try to rate a man on "ability to hold his temper" as an abstract item. On the other hand if he's slowing things up, or failing to get results on his job, and the cause is his temper, then this becomes a legitimate item of discussion by the coach. The emphasis is of course on the poor performance, and the coaching on how to change (control his temper) grows directly out of a performance failure. It's rooted in objective facts, and not in opinion or prejudice of the coach.

9. *Coaching requires rewards and punishments.* Building a hard-hitting team comes from high motivation of the employees on it. The first requirement is that people be told when they are doing a good job, and given some intangible and tangible rewards for exceeding what might be expected in the job. Monetary incentives—especially in business—are important motivators. Although used with more economy, reprimand and discipline are important motivators as well, and must be used without compunctions where they are clearly indicated in order to protect the team from decline in performance. The size of the incentive may have an effect on the improvement which can result. *Personnel* magazine, in an unsigned article in January of 1958, estimated that a range of 3 to 5 per cent has no incentive effect, and recommends a minimum figure of 15 per cent in order to have an appreciable impact.

10. *Man-boss relations are the key.* When a manager sets out to do a better job of moving his people into effective behavior, the success or failure of this effort will hinge upon the quality of the relationship between superior and subordinate. This isn't always everything it should be. Psychologist Irwin Taylor once surveyed 138 middle managers and found that most of his respondents received less time and attention from their boss than they felt they needed, that such talks when held weren't too helpful, that instruction rather than praise or criticism was the main reason for such get-togethers, and that few supervisors could actually help their sub-

ordinates since they seldom observed them at work. What did supervisors want their bosses to tell them? Most often it was something about the quality of their work, and their work methods. Taylor concluded this from his study:

> Before embarking upon a frenzied hunt for a program, companies would be better advised to see to it that their senior executives are provided with time and trained to use the tools needed to carry out the basic managerial function of developing their successors.

Still another student of the subject of coaching, Mr. D. E. Balch, formerly vice president of personnel for General Mills, has put it this way:

> Coaching requires that the man being coached know that his boss holds him in high regard, or the coaching won't work.

Here's how one sales manager reported his highly successful coaching program:

> When I took over the Northwest territory it was a sick region. The previous manager had violated every rule possible and most of the good men had left. Before swinging the axe I made up my mind that I would try to make these present people perform better than they thought they could. I started in by getting to know each man personally and intimately. I met their families, studied their records. I sized up their real capacities, and started working on making them better than they thought they were. It was slow work in the beginning. Finally one month we came through with the highest volume and profit for the country. You never saw such an elated bunch. I worked my tail off, coaching, showing, cajoling, eliminating unnecessary steps, increasing the number of calls per day per man, tying into advertising and merchandising promotions and all the rest. But the results were worth it in the rejuvenation these guys had when they saw that they weren't really the duds their former boss kept telling them they were.

Getting Subordinate Coaches to Coach

For the manager who has gone up through the organization and is in the general management level, coaching presents unique challenges. For one thing he's got to be coach of a more highly talented and able group than many who are lower in the hierarchy. Not that the lesser people aren't as smart, but the higher level people generally have more experience and knowledge of the company and its products. They've also been through some successful experiences and a screening process which brought them up to their present position. Therefore they rightfully feel that they need less coaching than the rookie at the bottom or the fellow whose only one step above the worker level.

For this reason also he may not have as much inclination to develop his own skills of coaching. As one such manager put it:

> I scrambled up through the pack, let the rest of 'em do the same thing. I believe in economic Darwinism and think that survival of the fittest is the best selection and development device for management.

In the depression days of the thirties, when managers of great capacity were often doing menial jobs, this indicated no need for extensive coaching. Yet the shortage of skilled managers for growth organizations today is an entirely different circumstance. Furthermore, technical changes in processes and products have made many successful managerial skills obsolete, and the demand for coaches in management positions today is more pressing than ever.

Coaching subordinates isn't an addition to a manager's job; it's an integral part of it.

Getting subordinate managers to become effective coaches of their subordinates in turn takes several distinct actions on the part of upper level management.

1. The top man must be a good coach and practice it. If the president takes time to work with his subordinates in coaching them, and letting them know that he expects that they will develop suitable replacements, then coaching will take place.

2. Subordinates follow their boss's example. Where the subordinate sees that he's being coached effectively he will not only emulate the coaching in practice, but will model his own coaching processes on those of his boss.

3. In some instances the recalcitrant may have to be told flatly that he's not doing enough coaching. When a general manager finds himself faced with outright resistance he may be required to talk cold turkey to his subordinate. In an eastern plant the plant manager was required, in the face of growth plans for the company, to tell his assistant:

> Look Fred, you know the business okay, and you are turning out the goods, but you aren't doing a damn thing to bring along any of the general foremen to take your place. All you ever tell me is how lousy they are. Yet you picked most of them, and you've supervised them for five to ten years. If they're no good who should I blame? I think what this means for you is that you sit your can on your chair and map out a good solid program of development for all of the general foremen, and come back to me when you've got it. I wouldn't wait over a month to do it either. . . . I'm going to be

talking performance review and bonus amount in three months and by damn this is going to be high on the list of things I want done, and you're going to have to get into the ball game.

Obviously such blunt talk isn't the first approach with most important members of the management team. Yet, when the circumstances demand it, it shouldn't be evaded.

Coaching subordinates is a business strategy and is one of the vital ways a manager makes things happen, not just in this accounting period but over the long haul.

11

How to Use a Personal Staff

"The attitude that 'the only way I can get anything done is to do it myself' is a dangerous one if the tasks referred to can and should be accomplished by a subordinate. Being busy is no virtue in itself— not if you're doing other people's work."

—*How Are You Fixed For Time?* SPIEGEL, INC.

You may be spending more time than you think in doing trivial chores. Perhaps you spend more time than you should in such things as making appointments, calling for meetings, or simply talking to people who could be screened by others. For the manager who makes things happen this choice of how his own time is used may be the key to the dramatic results he achieves. Yet many managers who find they can't get done the things they would like are surrounded by personal staffs of secretaries and assistants who, on the surface of things, would appear to be more than adequate to relieve him of all but the most vital of decisions.

In managing this retinue, the manager finds himself with several distinct problems which he must cope with if he's going to get the important jobs under way and show the over-all results his business needs.

Your old time stereotype of the executive who grabs telephones, sends minions scurrying about like chickens before a Greyhound bus, whose principal skill is pushing buttons that summon frightened subordinates onto the mat is extinct in most companies, as Auren Uris of Research Institute of America has put it:

> If he did exist, he owned his own business. It's doubtful that such an operator could long remain in the modern business organization where executive behavior is, to a large degree, social behavior.

Not long ago I talked to ten general managers about the use of their personal staffs. All of them agreed that this skill was essential for the top man in a division or company who was to get anything done at all. As one of them described it:

> It's a darn ticklish thing, running your personal staff. You see, I've got two basic sets of relationships. One set of relationships is with my subordinates who have great responsibility and authority for running the major segments of this division. These are the sales manager, production manager, personnel manager, engineering manager, comptroller, and traffic manager. They certainly aren't to be treated as if they were extensions of my arms and legs. They're strong and self-sufficient people with decision making powers of their own. Then there's another group that immediately surrounds me that's far lower in rank and pay, but who are vitally necessary to run my immediate office, and be my hands and feet in just getting all the things done that I can't take time—mechanically—to do myself. This personal staff can make or break me. They include my secretary, a clerk, my personal "assistant to," and a confidential clerk.

What these men told me can be summarized this way, when it comes to running this personal staff.

1. *They've got to be hand picked.* One of the general managers told me about the time he'd inherited a secretary who didn't like him, and whom he didn't like. Things went from bad to worse and he found himself getting mad over her behavior, and it sometimes carried over into his relations with the major executives in his division.

> Suddenly it dawned on me that I was a fool to continue what was obviously an unsatisfactory situation from both her viewpoint and mine. I had her assigned to another executive with whom she got along fine, and then I carefully chose another girl who seemed to suit my temperament better. Things were much easier for me after that.

2. *Close personal contact.* Although a major executive might well be able to remain aloof from some people, it's almost impossible to function effectively without establishing warm and congenial relations with the personal staff. An interest in them as people, and attention to the normal courtesies is imperative with a personal staff. It may be true that "no man is a hero to his secretary," yet it's necessary that he not become an iceberg with people who have the most frequent personal contacts of any person in the organization.

3. *Keep them informed.* One of the major requirements of using a personal staff is to keep them informed. Since they'll inevitably be handling confidential information, it's necessary to emphasize the need for a tight lip. It's quite pointless however to expect them to assist in the management of the personal office of the manager without being aware of what they need to know in order to get the job done.

4. *Know what they're doing.* **One** of the basic requirements of the manager in using his staff is to know just who is doing what.

> I discovered that some decisions were being made by people in my office who shouldn't have been deciding such big issues. It grew out of my lack of familiarity with what each general responsibility each one had. I clarified it and made certain that the major policy things came to me.

5. *Make them adapt to you.* **The** prime requirement of a person serving on a personal staff is that he or she be flexible in adapting his work habits to those of the executive. Certainly it's a major mistake to do the reverse.

> One section head in an advertising department found that he was altering his dictation practices to suit the schedules proposed by his secretary. This was perfectly okay until one day he discovered that he wasn't getting his letters out on time, and wasn't operating at peak effectiveness.
>
> "I'm always open to suggestion," he said, "but we changed back to my pattern instead of hers, to get my work done better. I guess she wasn't too happy about it."

6. *The boss should "shoot"—the staff set up targets.* **On** the rifle range while the expert riflemen are shooting in competition, down behind the target in a pit are men pulling targets. This analogy would fit into the use of the executive's personal staff. He's responsible for the shooting. It's the staff's job to set up targets and pull them down. Here's some of the things a personal staff might be doing for the boss:

> making travel reservations
> posting regular reports
> filing
> placing long distance phone calls
> opening and sorting mail
> setting up conferences with other executives
> initiating letters which require no policy decisions
> seeking out information
> writing speeches
> maintaining appointment schedules
> preparing travel agenda
> obtaining dossiers on people with whom contact is planned
> office maintenance
> screening callers
> operating ticker files
> prepare daily schedules for executive
> report information which he needs but doesn't have

initiate thank you notes and other customary amenities
issue reminders to the boss to follow up.

7. *Make decision areas clear.* The boss should make it crystal clear to his staff on what sort of decisions he will make himself and which he expects to be made by the staff. Generally, in those things on which there is a policy the staff may respond by stating the policy. Where there is no policy or its application is unclear these matters should come to the manager.

> The manager of a large leather plant found that he was achieving a reputation of being inaccessible since he had taken on an assistant-to. The reason he discovered was that the young man holding this position was injecting his personal judgment into problems, rather than carefully applying the boss's judgment as he himself would have decided it. The boss withdrew this right to engage in such contacts until the assistant was better acquainted with his philosophy and policy framework.

The important point here is that the personal staff of a manager isn't designed to be an independent decision-making group. They are expected to show great initiative, but always within the framework of "what would the boss decide if this matter were presented to him personally."

The best personal staffs have the capacity of even making their secondary use of the boss's authority bear the stamp of the boss's personality and managerial style. One speech writer said:

> My job of writing a speech is well done when the executive reads it and says that "it sounds like me." In one case I was required to prepare a speech for a man whose thinking was diametrically opposed to mine. I wrote it in such a way that the executive told me, 'I like this, you think the same way I do.' This was not the case. It did indicate to me however that I had captured the man in the speech I'd written for him, and that's my job.

Not everyone can serve as a personal assistant. This willingness to subject our own whims, likes, and individuality to that of the master pattern isn't possible for many people. If such is the case it's better for both the individual and the boss not to have such people on his personal staff. Internal conflict and discord between the manager and his assistant will result. One psychologist put it this way:

> In screening a man to be an assistant-to for a long period of time I generally try to find someone who has great intelligence and wit, but who hasn't any stamp of leadership ability in the old fashioned sense of the individualistic leader. Frankly, to be a good executive secretary or personal assistant requires the personality of a chameleon.

Your Secretary Can Double Your Efficiency

Most managers have a single secretary as their personal staff. For that reason it's vital that this important person be carefully selected, trained, and utilized. For the man who knows how to make the most use of his secretary, his personal effectiveness can be doubled, in the opinion of some experts. This entails some preliminary diagnosis before selecting, or re-training your secretary.

The first step is to identify what kind of manager you are yourself. Then you can describe what qualifications your secretary should have, or what work habits she should develop to get you further along in personal productivity.

Let's assume that you are by nature a detail man. You love checking the minutiae of the work of your department. Your secretary then should have the soul of an FBI man when it comes to patiently seeking out and obtaining information which you'll want for your decision-making processes.

On the other hand you may be a "big picture" man. You like to operate with sweep and a wide scope. Better have a girl who is good on details and will pick up all the little loose ends and do them for you without being reminded, or even caring whether you know she's covering up for your indifference to the fine points.

Or perhaps you're still another type or a combination of them. The first step in selection of a secretary is to find one who bolsters you up in the places where you are apt to be weakest in management of your office, and who complements your strengths through similar strengths of her own. One manager, a noted charmer, said this:

> I get my best results by selling people rather than hitting them over the head. I picked as my secretary a young girl with a winning smile and a warm friendly manner, both in person and over the telephone. Everybody agrees she's part of the office scene in my office because of these qualities.

Train Your Secretary to Your Work Habits

Once you've sized up the kind of executive you are, you're in a position to start training your personal staff and especially your secretary to adapt her pace and style of working to you. Here's how the vice president and general manager of an agricultural products firm did it:

> I once had a new secretary who'd worked in the pool and her work standards—especially on quality—didn't come up to what I wanted to come out of my office. I cogitated on it for awhile; then I began rejecting letters with errors in such a way that she had to type them

over. Being a bright girl she caught on that haste made slow progress and a startling improvement in quality came about. Now I know this isn't a universal tool of managing but in this case it worked beautifully.

For the manager who wants to enlarge the responsibilities of his secretary, here's what another manager has done:

> I began to turn out a volume of work which kept her at least half a day behind at all times. Then I'd pick a single job which was new and bigger for her. I'd call her in and teach her the new job—maybe setting up and maintaining some new control log I wanted to establish. She very shortly found that she could do a lot more of the routine stuff faster in order to get at the "project." Most office employees don't get "stretched" and accordingly don't enlarge their skills and capacity. Simply pitching more of the same stuff on top of the pile won't do it. You do this by adding on interesting and challenging jobs that flatter their intelligence. As a result the volume and quality of routine work gets done better too.

The concept of "job enlargement" or adding to the circle of responsibilities of a secretary until she has reached her full potential is a definite source of aid and assistance to a manager. This requires some careful scheduling of these new aspects of the job, and patient training until they are under control by the learner. Such methods add greatly to the satisfaction which the secretary gets from her job, especially as the lesser skillful demands on her time shrink proportionately.

There's one warning in all this, however. When you enlarge the responsibility and function of your secretary, don't be penurious about her pay. If she's carrying more responsibility and doing more of your personal work, make certain that she's compensated for the added demands on her better skills.

One of the obvious ways in which a secretary's time and your own can be conserved is the use of dictating equipment. I surveyed two groups of executives at the general manager level in two management development programs not long ago, on how many used dictating equipment instead of calling the girl in with her pad. Less than 30 per cent of the groups used a machine. The advantages in using such equipment in making the most of your secretary are something like this:

> She isn't duplicating your talking time—she's working from the machine while you're dictating the next memo.
>
> She can take verbal instructions from you even when you aren't there.
>
> The machine can be talked to at odd hours.

You can give your secretary instructions and correspondence even when you aren't in the office by mailing tapes.

Even though you waste time in dictating, she won't waste that same time, nor will she waste time transcribing since she can work at a uniform pace from the machine.

You can read your correspondence and dictate answers as they are finished without tying up the stenographer while you read.

Such machines require, however, that you be more articulate and precise in your dictation, since the secretary can't ask the machine for a clarification of what you mean. There are other limitations upon the machine. On the whole, however, it is a source of personal effectiveness which should be capitalized upon in using your personal staff.

Your secretary, like your subordinates, should be sent out of the office at least yearly for added training or information. Memberships in professional societies in the form of dues payments and expenses for dinners are a small investment when such activities can—through better secretarial performance—improve the manager's performance. The National Secretaries Association, in collaboration with a number of universities including Rutgers, Michigan, and Hunter offer special seminars and conferences for executive private secretaries. The topics for such meetings include human relations, public relations, grammar and spelling, systems and procedures, and basic management principles. All of these skills can be put right to work making your office run more smoothly and with a greater volume of work put out. It's a double advantage that you can improve your own effectiveness without personally attending the training sessions by which this improvement is effected.

What Assistant-to's Can Do (And Can't Do)

There are several practical rules in making the most of the "assistant-to" a manager.

1. He shouldn't duplicate or assume secretarial duties. The type of assistant-to who serves merely to pick up the miscellaneous duties which the boss isn't especially fond of normally ends up as being over-paid and very hazy in his usefulness. Such duties should be handled through added secretarial staff if they are absolutely too much for the boss to handle.

2. The assistant-to is the most logical way of handling new and special projects for which no permanent organization spot has been decided. For example, when the general manager finds that his public relations responsibilities are piling up and he isn't certain he's ready to move into the establishment of a public relations department, he may designate a man

to be his assistant-to to handle this function for him. Later if the function continues to exist and function, and the rest of the organization agrees that it should fit into some definite niche it may be transferred.

In some companies new technology such as the computer, operations research, organization planning, or profit improvement may be temporarily placed in such a category.

British consultant Lyndall Urwick describes the job of the assistant-to as being:

> Study, research, analysis, recommendation and above all to help his chief get things done by handling the publication of instructions, etc., watching the organization and foreseeing and forestalling any failure in coordination between the specialists and the line. He has no executive duties.

Basically the assistant-to should relieve the executive of his work. He should do the dog work in planning and controlling which the executive initiates, pulls together the use of outside advisors, and in addition to this he's being trained for greater responsibility elsewhere in the organization.

Yet this laudable goal isn't accomplished without some limitations on the use of the assistant-to. Because he's more than clerical or secretarial he may become invested with special power. Ernest Dale has pointed out some of the ways that people without delegated power may obtain it nevertheless. These include:

> power through superior verbal skills
> command through technical competence
> command through status (he's next to the boss)
> command through sanctions (won't send your report on in)
> command by default (the boss lets him make decisions for him)

None of these require an ounce of authority to command since they are based upon the willingness of people to act as if he actually possessed such powers through either misconception or cupidity. The assistant-to may find himself actually assuming authority because he's asked to take the posture of expert, or boss, or simply because he fills a situational need for others in the organization who don't have either his verbal skills, technical know-how, access to the boss, or access to the information which clusters about the boss's office.

In the light of this possibility it becomes important that the manager who wants to make maximum personal impact on the organization in favor of action and growth understand exactly how much influence and imputed command the assistant-to is wielding. Not to keep in touch with this trend can lead the decision-making not necessarily of the boss's making growing up gradually.

> Perhaps one of the most effective users of the staff assistant was, during his terms in office, President Eisenhower. Staff assistants, numbering as many as half a dozen in his case, screened every message, report and visitor according to general instructions and implied objectives of the chief. He read in detail things which his staff assistants stated that he should read, and accepted their word on what was contained in other reports. Through this means he was enabled to keep briefed on wide ranges of topics, and had access to the rest through the people who remained briefed upon them.

In one large manufacturing company it was found that foremen were spending up to five hours a day handling clerical duties. The obvious effect of this was that employees on the machines weren't seeing their supervisor and he was losing touch with his department. A combination relief operator and manufacturing clerk was assigned each foreman, and he was freed to inspect, train, and observe within his department. The savings were great since it freed the higher paid foreman from lower grade work and allowed him to bring his special supervisory skills to bear on improving the operation of his department, and improving the performance of all of his people.

Some of the things which assistants can do include:

> digesting material and reports received
> keeping situations under surveillance and reporting problems
> handling lesser visitors
> detailing in the broad plans laid down by executives
> establishing procedures for executive time
> making "trial balloon" statements to test reactions
> planning meetings and conferences
> making out schedules and detailed plans
> analyzing data received and pointing out important facts
> answering routine correspondence
> handling certain public relations functions
> managing administrative chores on "campaigns."

Effective Use of Executive Time

Bill Mitchell, vice president of General Mills chemical division, runs a small but profitable division of the larger firm in Kankakee, Illinois. As he puts it, he finds it necessary to perform many duties which would be assigned to another individual if the business were three or four times bigger than it is. Since these matters are so diverse and range through sales, production, laboratory to public relations that he treats it as extremely important that each subject be organized not only in his own mind but in the files of his secretary.

> At the close of each day, five minutes is set aside for review by writing down each major item which has been dealt with during the day. I also list those items on which more than one hour has been spent. In this way I find that sometimes I have spent considerable time on relatively unimportant items. I then place on the calendar for the coming day three or four principal objectives, and then matters which are of lesser importance.

Time is probably the greatest investment the manager has. Human power and effectiveness grows out of effective use of the time, and the treatment of time—especially his own—with respect. If he has a clearly defined purpose, and develops the skill to attain it he's developed a valuable asset for his company.

Here's a checklist which one executive developed for his personal use in improving his own utilization of time. You might want to try it yourself:

————Could any of the things I did today have been done in less time when I do them again? How?

————Did I use all the shortcuts available?

————Did I take on the tough jobs first?

————Did I wait for others to do something I might have done within a few seconds myself?

————Did I get wrapped up in something lengthy which I could have asked someone else to do?

————Did I fail to make a project clear to someone, thereby making it likely I'll hear a lot more about it later?

————Did I leave a lot of half done projects half way through?

————How much time did I lose due to procrastination?

————Did I keep my secretary fully programmed when I was away from the office?

————Did I tax my staff assistant with big enough jobs?

————Did I keep my energy level high by relaxing occasionally?

————Was I punctual for all my appointments?

————Did I fill in my idle waiting time with useful work?

————Did I waste any of my meeting time?

————What's the first thing I should do tomorrow?

From such a checklist it's sometimes easier to identify those things which a manager is doing which can be assigned another.

Perhaps the most helpful principle for using a personal staff is the "exception principle." Under this principle only the big issues are brought to the manager's personal attention, while the routine, repetitive and pot-boiling activities will be handled without specific managerial direction to do so by the personal staff. In order that no unduly bad effects result, a control system is set up whereby the unusual, or "exceptional" problems and occurrences will come automatically to the attention of the manager.

The development of procedures and systems to effect this feedback is part of the manager's job. In establishing the routines of his own office, it becomes important that he think "systems" in which information which reflects the larger organization he manages will be handled in routine fashions with only the new, the significant, and the important getting his personal attention.

This entails two things:

1. The manager must have a team of trained assistants who work closely with him to effect the results he wants.

2. This team must be governed by some carefully designed and smartly motivated and trained people to execute the plan.

12

Using Competition to Spur
the Organization

"The concept that appears to be emerging . . . is the concept of the team. It is an old concept but it is being put to new uses. As a member of the team an individual can find full opportunity for self expression and still retain a dynamic relationship to other individuals and their common assignment. This concept can, of course, be gutted by bad management—and has been on certain high speed production lines. But where it is applied with respect for the individuals that compose the team, it constitutes a new social technique of enormous power for all concerned."

EDITORS OF FORTUNE, *USA—The Permanent Revolution*

When Europeans come here on junkets to study the American character and return to their native land after three weeks, armed with complete data for analysis, they universally report one facet of our character. We work hard and play hard. After a stiff day in the office or factory we often return home to work equally hard at "do-it-yourself" projects in our cellar or expansion attic. Over the weekend or on vacations we drive three hundred miles to ski, or water ski in season. We play 27 holes of golf on Saturday, climb mountains on our vacations, or crank the mimeograph machine all evening for the PTA.

"I wish to preach not the doctrine of ignoble ease," said President Teddy Roosevelt, "but the doctrine of the strenuous life." His words would fall on ears as receptive today as they did around the turn of the century.

This passion for activity—sometimes just to be doing things—results in a general climate of competitiveness in business and the community generally which is important in understanding and motivating people at work.

A. C. Spectorsky has described graphically the vigorous manner in which exurbanites approach leisure. The rule seems to be that off the job and around the house the pace must be maintained, and the people across the street in the imitation Cape Cod mustn't be allowed to get ahead of us.

Whatever the social significance of these things may be, it's important for the manager to know, and especially if he's interested in human behavior, because he hopes thereby to move people into action on behalf of his organization.

This *new competition,* as we see it through the eyes of the manager, is somewhat different from the old style competition taught us in freshmen economics in college. The old style classical economics has a lot of different assumptions, which we now know—through the studies of social scientists—are neither correct nor appropriate as a guide to management decision making and policy. Take for example the basis of the old style economic competition; John Stuart Mill once wrote that, "In the case of most men the only inducement which has been found sufficiently constant and unflagging to overcome the ever present influence of indolence and love of ease, and induce men to apply themselves unrelaxingly to work for the most part in itself dull and unexciting, is the prospect of bettering their own economic condition and that of their family."

Whether or not this was true in the nineteenth century when Mill was alive isn't pertinent. It's more important to note that we've discovered some additional insights into human motivation since then, and the smart manager uses these new insights to get action from an organization.

It's equally pertinent to note that the competition which made up the engine of classical economics—being a kind of invisible hand which kept people efficient—doesn't work exactly the way Adam Smith and David Ricardo pictured it around 1800. Modern competition isn't ordinarily price competition, and the workings of supply and demand in the classical sense is more of an academic exercise than a description of the way competition works in reality. Nonetheless, competition as a moving force in business is just as vital—if in a different way—as the economists of the last century pictured it. Competition in modern business does the following things:

> It brings about a demand for innovation
> It spurs research and development
> It is the core of modern advertising and merchandising
> It is more often rooted in quality than price
> It is based upon service rather than cost to consumer
> It forces people to work more closely in teams
> It sharpens individual rivalry between teams

It demands that individuals stretch themselves to hold their positions
on the team for which they serve

It brings about the downfall of inept team leaders

It emphasizes cooperation between rivals for position

It's conducted without hostility being openly expressed

It places great demands upon individual performance of team members
to produce for the team

It demands special skills of conformity to the team's goals.

The Results of Healthy Competition

Because it has this different complexion it offers some fruitful opportunities for the manager who wants to make things happen in his organization. If he clearly understands the way competition works and the good results which come from skillful fostering of competition, his results can be phenomenal. Let's look at the case of a large food company which was faced with a serious problem.

> The manufacture and sales of baking mixes is a rigorous business in which competition is for *simpler* mixes for the housewife. She obviously isn't too interested in low cost alone or she'd continue to buy big sacks of flour, cans of lard, baking powder and so on, and make her own cakes like grandmother did. She'd rather buy a box of cake mix which is practically foolproof in the kitchen, and pay more to get the simple methods of baking. How does competition work here?
>
> Competition becomes a twofold process. The first place where competition enters is between research and development people in the labs and research kitchens. The end of such research is a more attractive cake, lighter, tastier, and easier to prepare with the chance of failure at a minimum. Once such a cake mix is developed the second competition is between marketing people who can write better copy, take more attractive photos, and create better images of gourmet cooking through methods of foolproof simplicity in the minds of housewives than those of the other companies doing the same thing.

Competition works here to pull all of the people in that company together for a grand assault on the problems of inventing and marketing a better mix. The research director and his staff vie with one another as well as their competitors in the other companies to come up with a better formula. The marketing people strain all of their creative talents toward preparing more appealing copy and art to tell this story that will move the housewife to reach for their product in the supermarket. They dig deep into human psychology, motivation research, as well as food technology and experimental cookery to produce the end product. Phd's in agronomy, engineering, chemistry, team up with artists, psychologists, statisticians, photographers, and printing experts to achieve the end result. To achieve such a dedication to a cake which can make it easier for the housewife to present her husband with as gastronomical masterpiece even though she spent the afternoon playing bridge, is the task of the manager of the entire activity.

To a large degree this result comes about because the manager has created the aura of importance which surrounds such work for the people involved in doing it. He makes the effort of each seem important by relating it to the internal necessity of meeting the competition of other teams in competing companies doing the same things as well or better. He isolates them from any questions or doubts which might be aroused in their minds about the world-shaking significance of better cake.

Most workers will respond more quickly to the challenge that "if we don't do it better, those other people will beat us out" than to any ideological arguments about vital importance of better cakes—or jet engines—to the world. Workers in defense plants during World War II were more often impelled to herculean records of production by the possibilities of breaking records, or beating out Lockheed or North American—or the crew on the next line—than they were about saving the world for democracy. Men in infantry platoons were normally more oriented to what the men in their platoon thought of their conduct in battle than they were about the ideology for which they had been drafted to defend.

The results of healthy competition, then, will be achieved more often through relating people to those in their immediate group than to some global and theoretical goal.

This isn't to say that the larger goal won't have an effect. People who have a larger goal that they can identify with, as well as a keen sense of personalized competition, will probably perform at closer to their maximum capacity than those who don't have such long range objectives. Yet, for the manager who wants to move his people into action most effectively, the basic problem over which he has control is this internal competition. Healthy internal competition *within the small group or between small groups* has these effects:

- It moves the members to put forth their best efforts
- It taps the latent abilities of the group
- It brings out the full energies of people
- It gives vent to their natural desire to be active and vigorous in their activities
- It springs creativity and productivity into full use.

Why People Compete

The deadly manager—the one who gets few results from his organization, who stirs up animosities and resentment—probably uses a few of the methods of the new competition in business. Often he's preoccupied with personal control, with exercising vetoes over the ideas and actions of others, and demands strict compliance with his wishes. This may grow out of ignorance on his part of the reasons why people in business enjoy competition.

People compete in business, and accordingly exert themselves far more than they might without this drive which energizes them, because it meets many of their needs. Here's some of the human needs which are met in business by competition:

It's interesting. The sad fact is that many jobs in industry are either dull, monotonous, repetitive, or trivial. People need to have their interests piqued by what they are doing in order to throw themselves fully into it. Ego involvement can come through doing important work. Yet, with the great rationalization of work into specialized tasks, it's nothing more than fact to say that most industrial jobs, including staff positions, are freighted with the possibility of colossal boredom. A manager can attempt to add interest to a job through several means. He can assure people that their work is important. He can tell them how they are a cog which can stop the whole machine. These have limited appeal. More importantly he can build interest into any job through getting ego of the worker attached to the results achieved. This almost always requires some element of success or failure being attached to the job. Competition is perhaps the most effective way of arousing this interest since it has little to do with the work itself.

The hope of winning. In the large business organization where the demands of simple management mean that people must be treated in standardized fashion, competition gains some special advantages. Where the worker becomes part of a competitive group he gains the opportunity to win special attention which seems to accrue to winners anywhere. The combative instinct, while not a dominant or even a basic one, is strong in our culture. It's ingrained in workers from childhood, and the prospect of winning makes the ardors of competition seem worthwhile.

The fear of failure. The other side of competition is that in pitting one's efforts or abilities against others in the group, or joining a group which is in competition with another group, there is a negative spur which prods the players on. The prospect of appearing less adequate than one's competitors, or of being laughed at, perhaps even of missing out on an award, can be a motivator that causes the worker to urge himself to heights of excellence and endeavor.

Using Recognition as an Action Getter

Keeping a competitive spirit alive in a group is best done through the adroit use of recognition as a motivator. What kind of recognition is best?

> A study by the Survey Research Center of the University of Michigan shows that both supervisors and employees agree that *pay* is the best form of recognition. The second most important form, employees declared, is training for a better job. Some of the commonly held views that praise, a pat on the back, or being called to the attention of supervisors are highly desired forms of recognition, proved to be not nearly as important as supposed by their bosses.

The United States Steel Company's "Creed of Human Relations" makes "recognition" its first specific principle.

Ed Boyer, executive vice president of General Mills lists five major reasons why recognition is an important tool for the supervisor or manager. These are:

1. It gives people a sense of belonging.
2. It prevents the same mistakes from happening again and again. This implies a recognition of bad work as well as good work.
3. People work harder and longer when they get credit for doing so.
4. Men grow through recognition—stagnate without it.
5. It requires that the supervisor know his business.

Competition of a productive kind grows out of the best uses of recognition. There are a number of ways in which a manager can use recognition to spur people into action.

> He can give them a raise or bonus
> He can tell them when they exceed the standards
> He can enter exceptional performance records in his personal file
> He can make public announcements of good performance
> He can train people for better positions
> He can tell his superiors about the achievement
> He can promote the best people
> He can give the man more responsible work.

Avoiding Unhealthy Competition

Despite the virtues which are implicit in competition to spur people to greater effort and higher quality work, there are methods of achieving competitiveness and types of competition which have a bad effect.

A large service organization had two major divisions, headed by two ambitious men. The general manager constantly played off one against the other. As a result the two were bitter enemies, and all of their subordinates took sides in the battle. Conflict, delay, confusion and lack of unity was the result. Service to the customers fell off due to this conflict and the overall organization suffered. In a large metal working plant the manager made it a habit to reward daily production records with immediate increases in pay, and was known to demote good men who had a bad run of materials or machine troubles beyond their control. As a result the foremen, who were able to make a good short run showing in production, quality, costs, spoilage, or grievances, got most of the good jobs. One man was known as a knife man, who would wring a department dry for a short while in order to obtain the praise of the manager. Over the long haul several costly maintenance jobs were required after he had left a department because he'd let maintenance go in order to make a good—but temporary—record for cost reduction. Everyone began to knife everyone else, and shove every possible expense over into the other fellow's department in order to make his immediate figures look good.

A chemical plant ran into troubles when the quality manager was prodded by his manager into "getting tough" with process supervisors over specifications and standards. As a result they reciprocated by trying the sneak through of some substandard shipments in order to "get even" and show him that they were smarter than he was. Several serious production mistakes followed during the year after that due to this competition to see who had the greatest authority. A staff department in charge of methods and procedures was urged to wring the costs out of several departments. They were told that the people there would resist them, but not to stop at anything, and if they had any troubles to fight back. As a result a grand feud began, and there was constant bickering and attempts to make each other look bad.

In each of these cases—which actually occurred—the competition had deteriorated from a healthy rivalry into cut-throat competition. The healthy instinct which causes men to pull together had aborted into a desire to get ahead oneself by making the other fellow look bad. There are several danger spots where sound competition can become unhealthy competition. Here's where a manager should keep his eye focussed to watch for such deleterious effects—and what to do about improving the situation:

Between partners at work. Where two equals are paired in a common task, it's possible that they will focus their attention upon beating upon one another, not in using the other's example as a stimulus to improving their own performance. The smart boss watches for signs of this inward turning between competitors, and squelches it promptly. Some of the first signs of it are when one begins to report the other's mistakes to the boss, or where he fails to cover up for the other and permits him to fail in the job. *The remedy?* Telling the two in no uncertain terms that this lack of unity between them is viewed as more serious than any failure of either to perform.

Between cliques. When informal groups having like interests band together to bring about the downfall of another group, the ill effects of competition can be painful to the company and the boss. Breaking them up doesn't always provide the answer. *The remedy?* Don't rush in too fast. Study each clique, its members, and the way in which they operate. What are the goals of the clique? Are there any common members between the two? Where the boss has acceptability to both he may appeal to the common members of both groups to bring about reconciliation. Failing this he may take a firm stand on any evidence of discord and indicate that he expects them to pull together in harmony. Perhaps the most useful method is to effect interchanges between groups. Getting them to *know* the other group and what is wants will often temper the hostility which is the immediate cause of the problem.

Between line and staff. Staff people may take a strong position and attempt to usurp functions of line management. Line people may ignore or even attack staff groups because they seem to threaten their position or function. *The remedy?* The first step is a clear definition of what line authority consists of and what staff's responsibility is. If the staff had advisory power only, this should be spelled out with some clear examples of how this advisory power is to operate. If they have functional authority to move in and make decisions (as in quality control in a pharmaceutical plant) this should be made clear as to both limits and scope. The line manager should be taught how to use the staff departments. Any evidence of conflict and competition should be explored by getting all the facts and explaining jointly and severally to the people involved what the rules of the road are.

Instilling the Desire to Win

Competition isn't alone as an influence that moves people to excellence. It's a strong one, but it's only effective when it's combined with a desire to cooperate—with the other members of a team, with the company as a whole, or with an individual. There are some tested methods which are used in instilling a desire to excel and to win.

1. *Let people know they're competing.* There's something stimulating and challenging in saying, "I'll race you to that corner" that adds zest to the trip. In all too many cases management doesn't let people know they are in competition or in a race, with the result that they don't extend themselves to win.

2. *Give an incentive to win.* The game must be worth the candle if people are to extend themselves. Often this may be merely a symbol. In one factory, for example, the foreman would buy coffee for the crew which came out best each day. The monetary amount was trivial, but it provided a symbolic, but tangible, means of rewarding the people who had extended themselves. Coffee or other small prizes won't work with many groups however, and something more substantial as an incentive must be applied. Perhaps the best form of reward and incentive is money, in the form of bonuses, or opportunities to advance where greater pay will result.

3. *Let people experience the benefits of winning.* With such incentives for excelling, it's only half the battle to quietly call the person aside and hand him his bonus or reward. Make public recognition of the winner through presenting his reward in a conspicuous fashion. This doesn't mean that the Michigan Marching Band must be brought to the plant every time a bonus is handed out. Sometimes simply listing these on a bulletin board, or mentioning them publicly where they would reach the ears of the less successful competitors, can have the desired effect. The more intense the competition, the greater the need for letting the victor bask in the glory of his victory.

4. *Ask for that little extra effort.* The benefits of competition and the desire to win to the organization, come through the little extra output which resulted in one person being top man. Nobody gets a prize for simply entering the race, although this has benefits too. He gets the prize for moving faster or smarter than the others who were entered, and who also ran. It's this little extra effort that gets the reward and moves others to attempt to put forth that extra effort next time. Making it clear through rewards that the sole reason for awarding first prize is that the person not only competed, but competed better than the others, is the core of using competition to get the extra results which are inherent in competition.

13

Effective Committees Can Pay Off

"A camel is a horse designed by a committee"
—ANON.

For the manager who is action-oriented the invention of the committee often seems like a device designed to thwart him in getting things done. Not only must he serve on many of them (one survey showed that the average general manager is on nine committees), but he frequently must manage the details of leading several. This is especially true when he works for a large organization.

Despite this general unease about the role of committees, he's probably created one or more in his time, and will probably create more in his career. One study by American Management Association showed that of 150 large companies surveyed, 110 reported standing committees as a regular part of their organization, with over 50 per cent having management committees which concerned themselves with problems on over-all administration of the firm. Others have functional committees which have general surveillance over policy in such areas as research, personnel, purchasing, manufacturing, contributions, public relations, and so on. The management committee may have an addition to its plenary group subcommittee, running to as many as five or six on a permanent or *ad hoc* basis.

When should a manager resort to committees to get things done? Basically there are six legitimate occasions for the appointment of a committee in order to make things happen more effectively than by any other method:

1. *To get participation.* When there are varied and possibly conflicting interest groups who will be affected by a decision or policies, appointment

of a representative from each involved group will provide a forum where dissents and viewpoints may be included in final policy *prior* to its being made. The obvious advantage here is that the latent opposition of conflicting groups can be ameliorated, circumvented, or eliminated by having representation upon a committee. A positive advantage lies in the ability of the various groups to contribute to the scope and ambit of the whole policy through their special knowledge of one facet.

2. *To bring about uniformity of direction.* It's almost inevitable that humans will differ on objectives and paths for reaching them if left to their own devices. These differences may have some advantages in originality, but they may also result in conflict between goals of the groups, and confusion and lack of unity in the whole organization. Committees serve as control devices for bringing the respective parts of the organism into line with the total objective through accomplishing some uniformity between the respective units represented on it.

3. *It trains the members.* The narrow specialist or the obstreperous person with selfish attitudes will grow through committee membership. There's an attrition into excessive individuality in an organization through committee membership, and the maverick may continue to be a maverick after long exposure to committee techniques, but he'll also be aware that others have equally strong views. Occasionally the strong member will change all of the others to his views where they are indifferent as to the decision being made, and in such cases will achieve uniformity of direction through giving in. In any event, the training experience from committee membership is a strong argument for its use. It brings not only knowledge, but has some effects upon changing attitudes as well.

4. *Strategically it packs more weight.* There's little doubting the strategic values of committees in complex organizations in terms of the weight which their conclusions carry. The board will be more apt to endorse a management committee action than a decision of an individual. For those down the line the fact that many people (a committee) has deliberated and decided, will make the final policy more palatable than a seemingly arbitrary decision of an indivdual.

5. *It's an effective morgue for foolish ideas.* For the action-oriented manager there's often an occasion when ill-advised, poorly timed ideas will need tactful disposal without the outward appearance of flat refusal. Committees, although costly for such purposes, are often a convenient manner of unloading and buffering the idea from seeing the light of day. While this buffer role of committees is more often used for bad purposes (killing

good ideas rather than bad ones) it has its place in the scheme of things for the action-getter too, as a means of handling tough inter-personal situations involving aggressive but wrong suggestions.

6. *It's a good repository for destructive criticism.* The manager who makes things happen is more apt to come under fire from his associates than the time server who simply keeps things at the status quo. Handling such criticism can be a time consumer for the action-getter, and a committee can serve as a convenient depository for such criticism.

> For example, one industrial engineering manager was making great strides with a cost reduction program, when several managers, made insecure by the program, protested that his program was disruptive to morale. The industrial engineer accepted these protests seriously, and asked several members of the protesting group to serve as a committee to study "in depth" the problem of how these considerations should be handled in installing the new cost reduction program. He promised to open his books to the committee and give them access to his files. The committee entered a lengthy but enthusiastic study of his entire program. After several months they came up with some minor suggestions for procedures, which he promptly adopted. Meanwhile the entire program had been installed and proved extremely effective in cost cutting.

When Individual Action Is Best

Despite these obvious tactical and managerial advantages in appointing committees, there are limits upon their appointment and usage. There are circumstances under which committees are both time consuming, inefficient and costly. Each circumstance should be weighed carefully to discover where the preponderance of benefit will lie. Since there will be advantages in both methods (individual and committee) in most circumstances, it may seem that the decision is moot. Yet, there are some guides when individual action is better in terms of getting action, without serious side effects which will undo the action taken over time.

1. *Individual action is best for directing action.* The organization principle of "one boss" is a sound one which is proven again and again in practice. Having an employee responsible to a committee is a multiple form of the evils of reporting to two bosses. Directions, orders, and discipline are best the matter of one leader. Action leadership tasks in the hands of a committee are almost always poorly executed, or executed with timidity, lack of resolution, and extreme caution.

2. *Innovation is rooted in individuals.* Committees and task forces who brain-storm may have certain valuable functions in solving jurisdictional.

problems, in communicating the information of the members to one another, and in overcoming future obstacles in execution, but the great creative work must be done by an individual working from his own insides. These creative acts occasionally are bettered by buffeting them around in committees, but many creative tasks are solitary. No committee ever wrote a great novel or painted a masterpiece. Yet it was a committee which created the Constitution of the United States. One format which can be used here is a combination of:

- the group meets and drops ideas which the creative man notes and fits into his thinking.
- the creative man does his innovating in private.
- he tests his creative innovation upon the group.

3. *Where immediate action is demanded.* For all of their virtues, the committees do not have great mobility and decisiveness. By their nature they are deliberative groups. In execution of decision and policy already decided, the individual is superior to the committee. This is especially true where speed of reaction is the essence of the situation. The football huddle, for example, is not a conference but an order giving situation. The shop foreman who is faced with a breakdown and the need for immediate decisions must have the power to direct others to move to positions of his choosing. The forcing of decisions down to the lowest possible level is based upon this principle, and group decision making under such circumstances can only result in what Admiral Rickover has described as "a train on which every passenger has a brake."

Who Should Be On a Committee

When "Engine Charlie" Wilson was made Secretary of Defense he called a meeting, it is reported, which he estimated should have brought forth six people, or ten at most. Over thirty showed up. Glaring around the room, he snorted:

"What are all these people doing here?"

At the next meeting, it's said, less than six showed up.

The point is that committees have a way of attracting people who have a natural proclivity for attending meetings, even when they aren't required.

Since committees and committee meetings aren't always the most productive place for a person to be spending his time, control over the number of people who are members, and equally stringent control over those who attend its meetings should be maintained. Some companies have done these things to control committee size, and attendance of members at committee meetings:

- Eliminate from membership people whose contribution or usefulness to the committee is only sporadic. Invite such people to attend those meetings where things that concern them are to be discussed.
- If the work of the committee is complex and might require the work of subcommittees, appoint members of subcommittees who are not members of the committee as a whole. The member of the full committee then reports back on the actions or recommendations of his sub group without necessitating their being on hand.
- Use "task forces" of staff people to do the work of committees with the proviso that they be discharged from the committee upon completion of the required staff work.

Who then should be included on a committee?

As a general rule, only those people who will make a contribution to the objective of the committee most of the time. Yet this entails some *caveats* if the effects of the committee action are to avoid disruption and require re-doing the work of the committee because it omitted some vital interest group. Here's some guide rules:

1. *Policy committees.* Membership on committees which can make or effectively recommend policy should include the chief manager of every department who must execute the policy. For instance, the salary committee should include the major executives of the divisions and staff departments who must abide by the findings of the committee. The result of not including such people is a failure to comply, with the justifiable excuse that they either didn't understand, didn't agree, or didn't believe that the policy applied to them. Others who might be asked to join or sit in on such meetings are people on "the verge" of top management who might acquire a feel for such deliberations by taking part in committee activity.

2. *Problem solving committees.* These are normally ad hoc committees established to do such necessary things as cost reduction, profit improvement, or other similar problem areas. Here the committee should represent the various areas of the business which must execute the plans developed, as well as some technical experts from staff departments which can provide expert analysis and advice on specific subjects such as accounting, industrial engineering, and so on. Such committees may be designed with steering

groups of top men, and temporary members to bring in special reports or perform special functions.

3. *Training committees.* Certain companies, such as the McCormick Company of Baltimore, have formed "junior boards" which serve to train their members in problems which have significance to the senior boards of the company. Members of such committees have ordinarily been selected for their potential advancement, and for their position as representative of certain functions or departments of the company. They deal with specific issues and make recommendations to the senior boards regarding policies which affect the lower echelons. Membership is rotated to permit as wide a distribution of the membership and training opportunities as possible.

One of the great plagues of the committee system is the use of committees as a means of drafting people to do extra work without adding them to their job description. University faculty committees, and occasionally such committees as employee recreation, junior achievement, fund raising, and similar peripheral activities are managed in this fashion. While they serve the purpose of getting free work, they frequently sap the time and energy of busy people in a way which places some doubt upon their ultimate efficiency. Perhaps a more efficient manner of handling such assignments would be to assign some full time people to performing the chores, and rating them on their performance in them. The ultimate cost in terms of man hours would be far less. As a cold, hard matter of personal career planning, such committees are to be avoided where such avoidance doesn't put one into direct violation of the stated desires of a superior. The ideal person for such committee work is the least busy, and perhaps the least able person. He is apt to find such activity pleasant and enjoyable, and a means of garnering honors and responsibilities which he might never otherwise obtain.

Keeping Committees Under Control

The Standard Oil Company of California and other companies have established systems of annually reviewing committees to keep them from becoming a great jungle which strangles the efficiency of the organization.

The manager who hopes to keep the fat from accumulating in his organization may find that such a procedure is worthwhile in his organization too. Here's a procedure for keeping the spawning of useless committees within reasonable bounds:

Draw up a committee organization chart. The first step in controlling committees is to draw up an organization chart of the *committees* which exist. One effective way of doing this is to start with the top nine or ten men in the company and ask them to prepare a brief memo stating what committees they belong to, how frequently they meet, and how many subcommittees each has. These can then be compiled into a master committee roster, and plotted graphically to show the overlap and duplication existing. This step in itself will suggest ways in which simplification can be made.

Then test each committee. This can be done by asking of each committee *what* is its purpose; *why* is it necessary; *who* is on it that might be eliminated; *when* does it meet; and is this the proper timing (does it meet too often); and finally *how* could the work of this committee be eliminated, changed, simplified, or combined with another. Such hard questions asked of each committee yearly will wring out some of the grossest cases of committee-itis in an organization and free executive time for more productive efforts.

Five Guides to Effective Management of Committees

In studying any single committee, or in studying the whole structure of committees, the manager who hopes to keep the organization vital and trim should look at five factors with regard to each committee:

- committee economics
- weighing committee contribution
- using the principles of group effectiveness
- it should have tight procedures
- it should deal only with "committee" topics

It might be worthwhile to explore each of these a little more in depth.

Committee economics. The costs of committee operation are often hidden, but are extremely high in most companies. A committee should be weighed against the out-of-pocket costs of secretarial help, of the salaries of those attending, and of time and space used. Beyond this, committees cost even more through poor execution of their decisions which might better have been made elsewhere, and the immunity to criticism which improves performance and inhibits sloppy performance. Often the committee is costly in the internal politics which it generates through its activities. In many instances this is because the "least busy" member of the committee, and perhaps the least well informed member, has the greatest influence because he has time to work at the busy-work of committee activity. This least busy member will ordinarily initiate more vetoes, and demand more by way of preventive action by managers than any other member. All of these costs should be considered in weighing a committee's effectiveness.

Weighing committee contribution. Placing a strict cost and profit analysis against committee output is probably impossible to do. Yet a general yardstick of profitability should be applied in every case. Does the committee contribute more than its cost in terms of training, in terms of problems solved, of acceptance gained for ideas and programs, of coordination of related functions, and of tightness and logic of policy? The committee system can hardly contribute to profit during the coming fiscal period, and it's often pointless to even attempt to evaluate it on this basis. It isn't impossible to ask, however, what the committee has added to the stability and growth potential of the firm through its actions in the current period. There are committees which have added immeasurably to these growth and stability factors in a firm. The facts are that there are good committees and bad ones, and the good ones have contributed to growth and stability of the social organization of the firm. The experienced executive must use his intuition and experience to evaluate the contribution. The standard is intangible, but is nonetheless real. Like individuals, committees may be subjected to performance appraisal. One useful standard is to ask how the committee performed against its *stated objectives.* Another is to ask for a listing of its contributions and weigh these against possible alternative ways of accomplishing the same goals.

The committee should use the principles of group effectiveness. Being a good committee leader requires experience and skill. It takes an equal amount of skill to be a good *member* of a committee. Courses and programs aimed at sharpening these skills are economically sound where the committee system is well entrenched.

Ernest Dale has spelled out some criteria which guides group effectiveness. They include some of the following:

- The members should have skill in verbal expression.
- Conflicts must be resolved by integration, not by domination on the part of a single member or the leader, nor by compromise which leaves both parties sullen about the result.
- Committees should emphasize the concrete and practical, and avoid the blue sky topics, the philosophical, or the speculative questions not solidly rooted in factual.
- Productivity in a committee comes through their being given urgent problems, the power to make decisions or recommenda-

tions, easy communication between the members, an orderly system of treating problems, and the intelligence and originality of the group.

- Agreement in committees, research shows, comes through strong attraction between the members for one another, through personal friendships in the group, through uniformity of background and interest, and the presence of few dissenters and mavericks. (The latter may not be desirable since a maverick may often bring in original ideas.)

Committees should have tight procedures. Every committee should have its scope and function defined clearly before it is allowed to function. It should be the proper size. Research at Harvard's Social Relations Department indicates that under five is undesirable and over 15 is unmanageable. Its chairman should be weighty in status and skilled in conference leadership. He should not dominate, nor should he be passive. The secretary should be chosen from among the weightier members, since his impact on the results through preparation of minutes is considerable. To get action from committee meetings the agenda should be circulated in advance, and other information related to decision should be in the hands of members in sufficient time for them to study the materials.

> "I never can think clearly in some committees," one executive reported, "because they throw things out I haven't had time to digest. They should send them out in advance."

In one company all committee meetings are scheduled one hour before lunch or before quitting time in order that the chairman will not let things wander, and the groups won't tend to drag things out. It's been found in this company that few meetings run over-time when they're scheduled this way.

Committees should deal only with committees' topics. The ideal topic for a committee is jurisdictional disputes. Here the manager can throw the dispute to the people who have been most heavily engaged in such disputes, along with some neutral figures. Under the duress of committee procedures and a firm charge from the person appointing them, solutions are often found with which the members will abide. Still another committee purpose which is beneficial and productive of unity is where people who have little opportunity to see one another in daily work schedules will become better acquainted and both formal and informal communication will be forced into being. This is a valuable function of a committee and in some instances is the major purpose of the committee. Policy making which entails both of the above problems can legitimately be identified as a good communication area. The topics to be avoided are:

- how to do something
- the administration of an activity
- the execution of a plan.

In short, committees can be vehicles for getting things done. They require careful planning and managerial control, if they are to become effective tools of the action-oriented manager.

14

The Gentle Art of Chewing Out a Subordinate

"Once the compass points north and we know where we're going we stay on the beam. I ain't interested in ideas that are off the beam, and I ain't interested in people that are off the beam. Check!"
"Check," went around the board table like a whipcrack.

—FREDERICK WAKEMAN, *The Hucksters*

There's a necessity for order in an organization if it is to survive, and perhaps even more demand for such order if it's to grow. This corporate discipline which brings about unity isn't a natural condition of human groups, and grows out of the behavior of its leaders. What leaders do to accomplish this unity, without running into counter facts and ultimate disunity because of *wrong methods* of establishing and maintaining order, is vital.

As Dr. Dallas Jones has pointed out, the new discipline in industry is substantially different from the type which prevailed when the manager acted as the overseeing agent of the owner. Under such circumstances the employment contract which every man entered into when he went to work implied that the boss was entitled to be autocratic in directing people who entered his premises. This tacit agreement was part of the entire package, and was a condition of employment.

Two conditions have brought about a major change of the disciplinary concept. The first has been *psychological-social* and presumes that it isn't always wise to exercise one's property rights in dictatorial fashion. The second is a new *legalistic* concept of discipline which requires administrative remedies (union contracts, grievance procedures and so on) which are available to the person who is treated unjustly at work. These two forces have combined to change the entire emphasis of discipline. The law which governs employees in the modern organization has little to do with putting down rebellions against property rights, or squelching impertinence.

Modern discipline aims almost wholly at bringing people in the organization into line with the "law of the situation" which is created both by the organization and its surroundings.

A Code for Management Discipline

The skills of chewing out a subordinate take on an entirely different coloration under this new code of discipline than that which existed in the smaller and more personally owned firm of the past century, and extending into this in many places. In brief, this code of management discipline (which governs reprimand procedures) goes something as follows:

1. *Discipline implies rules, not personal desires.* Conformity in the directives of immediate superiors is in part a requirement of discipline. They are not the entire aspect of discipline, nor are all directives consistent with good discipline. Gordon Rattray Taylor has set up a requirement for leadership that the legitimacy of the leader must be acknowledged by the governed. This means the leader must clearly show that he has a right to be in charge. The old expression "rule of law, not rule of men" is another way of putting it. Mary Parket Follet expressed it as being the law of the situation. The rules, under this concept, are not arbitrarily designed to please one man, but are patently required for the organization to get where it wishes to go.

2. *Discipline implies correction of error in a situation.* The manager who objects to what is proposed or has been done or said, assumes the responsibility to propose and perhaps to execute himself something else which he substitutes. Carping and criticizing for purposes of destroying the other's initiatives, or simply telling him he is wrong-headed, places the manager in the position of spectator, rather than active participant in the game. Here's how one large company president put it:

> With my major officers I know that their decisions are really choices among several alternatives which they have considered. For me to impose my choice in preference to theirs also means that I'm assuring personal responsibility for the skill with which the decision is executed. I'd be foolish to do that. I therefore limit myself to asking pointed questions which assure me that all alternatives have been considered. Once that's done I step back and let them go ahead with their own decisions.

3. *The best discipline is situational authority.* The manager who steps into a situation with authoritative manner and directs changes with added comments upon the qualification of the person who is doing the job, in effect relieves that person of his post—temporarily or permanently. On the other hand where he is merely suggesting and the suggestion can be— and has been upon occasion—rejected by the subordinate, the discipline is healthy and sound for the organization. For example, the comments of subordinates upon superior's work will often be in this category since its tenor is normally carefully designed to avoid attacks upon the person, and limited simply to the presentation of special knowledge and insights into the demands of the situation.

4. *Discipline shouldn't damage delegation.* When the manager "chews out" the subordinate in a manner that indicates that he intends to substitute his judgment wholly for that of the subordinate, the cause can usually be traced to some personal pique. Either he considers the offender as impudent or impertinent to him ("he's insubordinate"), or it's an ego-protection device for the whip wielder. He sees the offender as a personal threat to him, or he feels insecure by the acts of such people and attacks them from the vantage point of his position of authority.

> Take the case of the personnel manager who made it a habit of walking around the plant and reporting any violations of regulations to the president. This was inevitably done by listing names of employees and their supervisors as well as caustic suggestions for action. The president, while not desiring to have regulations flouted, advised the personnel manager to "report bad situations to supervision involved, and avoid personalizing your approach."

The emphasis in sound discipline must be on *what's wrong* rather than *"who's to blame."*

5. *Discipline must entail equity.* Even the youngest child reacts unfavorably to anything which seems to smack of injustice. Favoritism, unequal application of the rules, discriminatory treatment, have immense capacities for arousing rebellion. People have gone to the barricades and laid their lives on the line to prevent injustice, and will undoubtedly go to great extremes to prevent it again. To the average employee fairness means the same thing as consistency.

6. *The discipline of system and method is least objectionable.* In circumstances where uniformity and conformity are desired, the best control over such behavior is to establish a uniform procedure, and to explain it. This means that people govern their behavior to fit the procedure, and

knowing that others have accepted the procedure will probably not find it onerous.

> In one sales organization each month over half the expense accounts submitted were rejected and returned for corrections or further information by the controller. Sizing up the situation, the sales manager printed up a new batch of expense forms, with detailed instructions for their completion on the bottom. Rejections fell sharply and the beginning of a feud was squelched. Nobody objected to following the procedure. They objected keenly to the personalized rejections without standards known to them in advance.

Reducing order-giving to mean "following a set pattern of behavior," as contrasted with the requirements of "ask the boss what to do" has numerous advantages in maintaining discipline.

- It alleviates the possibility of personal affront to the boss because his "orders" weren't "obeyed."
- It eliminates the possibilities which constantly exist of routine direction being freighted with pique or innuendo that creates resistance.
- It helps remove some of the emotional difficulties which grow out of one man's resentment of another man having power over him.

This doesn't mean that personal contact between the subordinate and his boss are always undesirable. On the contrary. Such contacts are to be sought after. They are most effective however when they are within the framework of coaching, teaching, giving assurance, reacting to questions, commending good performance, or establishing personal rapport which indicates the regard of one person for the other.

7. *Discipline should never rob a man of his dignity.* Most arbitration cases over discipline are based on inequity or loss of self esteem on the part of the employee because of the manner in which the disciplinary action was taken. The famous instance of President Truman removing General of the Army MacArthur from his post aroused a national emotional binge simply because "of the way it was done." Even those who felt that MacArthur might have been insubordinate to his commander-in-chief were aroused at the indignity in the method of his removal. This indignity lay in the stature of the man, his past contributions, and his sincerity in his desire to serve his country. The lessons for managers are clear. No single defect or act merits disciplinary action which leaves the man no dignified way of retreating to a position where his status and manhood are preserved.

Some commonly held Rules which every subordinate believes to be his due include:

- The right to privacy when being reprimanded.
- Freedom from "entrapment" in which a situation is deliberately rigged which will cause him to do something that invites discipline.
- The making of an example of an otherwise innocent and one-time offender while flagrant violators are, by chance, allowed free with lesser penalties.
- The varying of the intensity of enforcement of rules. Where violations of rules have been condoned, bad effects upon morale will follow a sudden and arbitrary tightening of the rules without notice.
- Attacks upon his personal worth for specific offenses. Where he makes an error he will concede the right of the boss to invite his attention to these mistakes and direct him "not to do it again" or even punish him, but he rejects generalized complaints and suggestions about his over-all lack of adequacy or worth.
- Inconsistency of treatment from time to time or among persons. Inconsistency may be the hobgoblin of small minds, but in terms of discipline most of us are small.
- Comments about performance which are only forthcoming when things go wrong, and never when good work is done. Recognition, as we've seen earlier, should cover both good and bad performance.

When to Reprimand

As in many of the arts, timing becomes of paramount importance in reprimanding a subordinate. Timing is probably one of the "skill" areas of management which only experience can develop, and the artful manager studies the matter of timing and notes which sequence of reprimands has the most effect in achieving the best results.

> Take the case of the research manager who went to his management with an idea for a research project that would be both pioneering and daring in its nature, and very costly. With some misgivings the approval was given to proceed. After spending more than twice his estimated budget the research manager was asked for a progress report. At this point he confessed that he had reached a dead end, and suggested that the project be abandoned. Management very wisely agreed without a word of protest or demand for explanations of his action. The man was being sufficiently wracked by his own

professional pride, and added reprimand or censure at that time would have been very damaging, and might have caused the man to leave. Since he was basically a sound man, they allowed the matter to be quietly dropped. A year later, under his direction, an extremely profitable project paid off more than enough to cover the original losses on the wrongly selected project.

There are numerous instances when reprimands are best delayed or withheld completely. Good managers who are aware of the standards of performance by which his job is measured often punish themselves more severely than any outsider could do. In some cases there may be a need for undisciplining.

Fred G. was general manager of a consumer product division of a large company which was offered a chance to market a new product. Under the pressure of day-to-day business, an incomplete investigation resulted in the offer being declined, with the result that the supplier took his product to a competitor, who made a great success of it. The chagrin and remorse of the first manager was so great that his president made a special trip to his home to assure him that nobody held this lapse against him, and to get on with doing the continued good job with the present line that he had been doing in the past.

Often it's the mistakes of omission about which we punish ourselves most, and for which managerial discipline and reprimand are least needed. These can be used as occasions for coaching and teaching, but to "nag" is nothing more than pointing out inadequacies of the past about which the man can do nothing.

Generally however, the timing of reprimands becomes one of deciding whether to collect several examples and do it for all of them, or to make an immediate reprisal. Generally the gathering of evidence is designed to make a more general case against a man to prove to him that he has some over-all deficiencies. This is often done when the man is being fired, and the specific incidents are collected and noted as evidence of a more general inadequacy which is sufficiently large to require his release. They may, of course, be accumulated for other purposes, for example to convince a man that he needs to drastically revise his behavior or attitude when the single reporting of an incident wouldn't have that effect.

In a large southern insurance company one of the better young sales managers had let success go to his head and was letting his performance slide. He often stayed home after heavy weekends, and was overly friendly with several female employees. The general manager in charge collected a number of specific incidents over six months and finally confronted him with these facts, plus some

verbatim comments that outsiders had made to him about the salesman's high living and apparent loss of his old abilities. Confronted
with this array of facts, the young man was appalled and promptly
turned over a new leaf.

In other instances it's valuable to take each specific incident and make
the reprimand immediately. As every parent knows an immediate swat
with a hairbrush by mother is more effective than the vague threat of "wait
'til Dad gets home." Distance and the possibility of future reprisals have a
diminished effect upon a person's behavior. This is especially true with
the new employee, and most especially with the young employee on his
or her first job.

One executive found that a new secretary was habitually late in
getting to work, and seemed happily oblivious to his broad suggestions that everyone in *this* office works eight hours a day. After
several such days he confronted her one morning coming in fifteen
minutes late, and ordered her quietly to go home for a week without
pay. After a week she came back and was a model employee.

Very often the timing of the disciplinary action can be made on the spot
and effective immediately, and inevitably the result will be a serious re-
thinking of the situation by the employee.

The Seven Deadly Sins of Reprimanding

There are some serious errors which a manager can make in reprimanding.

1. *Failure to get facts.* Be sure you have all the facts before leaping.
Don't accept hearsay evidence, or go on general impressions.

2. *Acting while angry.* Don't act while you've lost your temper. Be
calm in your own mind, and as objective as possible in making a decision
to reprimand. Ask yourself, "Is it possibly my fault that the error or violation occurred?"

3. *Let person be unclear of offense.* Let the person know the general
charge, and the specific details of the offense. Don't allude to general complaints, or refuse to give details.

4. *Not to get the other person's side of the story.* Always let the persons have their full say about what happened and their reason why they
did what they did. There may be mitigating circumstances, conflicting
orders, or even orders you gave unclearly which were at fault.

5. *Backing down when you are right.* Compromise and understanding
are virtues, but once you've decided and announced your decision it is a
mistake to relent. It merely indicates you were wrong in your first decision,
and you'll lose the effect of your reprimand.

6. *Failing to keep records.* Disciplinary reprimands should always be recorded in the personnel folder of the person. This becomes part of the work history of the person and provides evidence in the event of further disciplinary requirements. In many cases people who were known to be unsatisfactory employees over the years have been reinstated after discharge because the company could produce no evidence that the person had ever been told of his shortcomings.

7. *Harboring a grudge.* Once the reprimand has been administered and any sanctions or punishments administered, don't carry a hostile attitude forever after. The person required discipline and received it. Assume now that they are starting with a clean slate and let them know that you consider it a thing of the past.

Reprimanding Without Losing the Man's Regard

We've seen that it's a mistake to reprimand a man in front of his colleagues. This doesn't mean either, that simply because it's private (and more personal) that anything goes in a reprimand.

Perhaps the most effective guide to maintaining the regard of the individual is to *know* the man you're dealing with. A raw beginner who is "just a kid" probably has a different image of what his relationship with the boss should be like, from the old and experienced hand who is used to being treated with some respect.

The key to effective reprimand is to fit the reprimand to the man's own image of himself.

Every person has self perceptions which may or may not be accurate, but which he obviously likes or he wouldn't have them, if he's normal. The wise supervisor knows his people, including how they see themselves. Let's see how this works in practice.

Harry B is a supervisor of mechanical departments and is generally a responsible, mature person. He takes his work seriously and is most conscientious in his planning and the quality of the work under him. He takes himself somewhat seriously and brings an air of importance to the things he does. Yet he failed to perform adequately when it came to installing a new system of labor control, and the plant manager wanted to let him know that he was dissatisfied. He called Harry's secretary and arranged an appointment for two days ahead. He arranged a private meeting, and collected all of the facts and data carefully. When explaining his dissatisfaction over progress to date he was straightforward but serious. No fireworks, no ranting or raving. He gave Harry ample opportunity to explain and talk things over. After securing agreement from

Harry to give the thing a more vigorous try (and agreeing to do certain things which would help) the two men shook hands upon parting.

There was no doubt in Harry's mind that he'd been hauled over the coals by the boss. Yet, since the boss treated him and the situation with the same seriousness with which Harry would have treated a lapse by a subordinate, no bad effects occurred. The system was installed in due course without further delay.

Another case was that of Carrol B who was an energetic young industrial engineer. Carrol was bright, able, and enthusiastic. He had a bright manner of talking, and was witty in his responses. He enjoyed a personal and informal relationship with his people, and with line managers. His boss was only a year or two older than Carrol and knew him very well. When Carrol slipped up on a job the boss's conversation was handled this way:

"Hello Carrol, this is Bill."

"Hello Bill, sounded like Richard Nixon."

"Nixon hell, I'm only a poor plant manager. Listen buddy, when you gonna get on the ball?"

"Which one?"

"The project ten ball, that's which one."

"Oh, that one."

"Yeah, that one. Look buddy, if you don't have something to show me on that by the end of this week, it's going to be you and me going around and around this building. You know who'll be in front?"

"I can imagine."

"What happened anyhow? New York office is raising hell with me on this job."

"I kinda let 'er slip I guess. How about something by Friday?"

"Could you?"

"Sure, anything for Richard Nixon."

"That's a promise, pal. If you don't have something then you'll be on the first rocket to the moon. This is hot, so put 'er up on your list of things not to goof off about."

As a result the project was pulled out and given some expert and rapid attention. In fact Carrol worked several evenings getting the project completed, and by Friday it was done. Because the reprimand was consistent with Carrol's self image, he hardly took it as a reprimand.

One of the greatest limitations in this technique is that it demands some perception on the part of the superior of how the subordinate sees himself. That this isn't always accurate has been shown in many studies. Dr. Lee Danielson has shown, for example, that engineering managers tend to see their subordinate engineers as *emotional* people, whereas few engineers see themselves this way. Danielson suggests that this may be due to lack of observation skills on the part of the supervisors, and also the fact that because so many of their contacts with their men are emotion-laden that they draw a distorted image. Yet even imperfect images, and using them to shape the form and style of reprimand, is better than ignoring this important facet of discipline. The stuffy individual would resent a flippant approach to reprimanding him as much as the more easy going one would be repelled by any attempt to "act like a big shot" over his lapse. The important point is in the result achieved, rather than in the method used. Asking the man or woman to change their behavior with regard to their job is one thing. Asking them to simultaneously change their personality and ways of adjusting to situations is another.

By fitting the method of reprimand to the image which the person has of himself, he frequently doesn't even see it as a reprimand in the conventional sense of the word. He stands corrected, and knows that he has failed to please, but doesn't feel that his integrity as a person has been violated. The range of such images is perhaps limitless. People see themselves as crisp administrators, beautiful maidens, hail-fellows, ivy-leaguers, egg heads, dedicated scientists, he-men, conservators of the business, as weaklings, and in one of a thousand other roles. Fitting the method to the perceived role the man plays, and making the reprimand method acceptable for the person in his role, is one of the tested ways of accomplishing the purposes of the reprimand without losing the man's regard.

Discipline Without Loss of Dignity to the Subordinate

Discipline problems are seldom ever created by acts or lapses of the moment, but over a length of time are the creation of the leader in his selection of subordinates. This is further accentuated by the training he gives them. It is further a product of the organization of work which he performs or fails to perform, and the ampleness of his planning the work to be done. Where these things—selection, training, organization, and planning—are skillfully done they will minimize the necessity for conventional chewing-out forms of discipline. Since there is understanding from the first as to what the situation demands of the member, there's far less incidence of situations which call for reprimand.

There are a variety of ways in which a man receives dignity from his superiors. The first is probably a simple cordiality in casual contacts. This cordiality often indicates a willingness to be friendly and helpful to the subordinate without going so far as to indicate total dependence upon him. The second major way in which men obtain dignity in their position as subordinates is through having superiors who help them succeed. By paying careful attention to his interests and helping him to accomplish them somewhat beyond what the man might expect accords dignity to the subordinate. On the other hand, arousing expectations of assistance from a superior and then not producing such assistance results in lost dignity for the subordinate.

This "set" or approach to management—the boss being the helper of the subordinate—has many concrete things to commend it in terms of results achieved. Perhaps the best practical way of doing it is to periodically sit down with the man and jointly work out the objectives of the man's job with him. Each contributes what he sees as the possible achievements during the period ahead, and they have a common ground upon which performance evaluation can be made other than subjective opinion of the superior. Yet such objective setting requires some additional steps from the boss.

- It requires that at the end of the specified period he sit down again and review with the man the actual accomplishments against the goals established.

- It requires that the boss ask himself privately, "What can I do, do differently, or refrain from doing, that would help this man accomplish his goals?"

The major advantage of this system of mutual goal setting between boss and subordinate is that it imposes a system of self-discipline upon each subordinate, and a means of measuring his own performance against the agreed upon goals.

In companies where this system has been tried on a large scale—General Electric, General Mills, Michigan Bell Telephone, and Merck and Company—the effects have been highly satisfactory. As an executive from one of these firms put it:

> I sit down with the boss annually and we work out my program for the year in every area of my activity—including some personal development for me. Throughout the year I have a ready reference on how well I'm doing against what my boss expects of me. At the end of the year we sit down again and work out new goals, and review how well I did on the past year. Yet, he doesn't have to sit in judgment on my performance because I can do that for myself. We're working from the same standards, you see ... we agreed on them in advance. If I muff a job that I agreed to do I don't have to wait for my performance review to learn about it. I have it in front of me constantly throughout the year.

The Decline of the Chewing-Out

Although there will undoubtedly always be a certain amount of reprimanding and bawling-out of subordinates as long as one man wcrks for another, as a general means of management it's on the decline. This is only in part because we've become more civilized and considerate. The principal reason is that new amenities that work better in getting people to excel in their work have proven more effective. More rational organization of work, more participation, and the breaking down of class and status systems carried into the work place from the outside, make temper tantrums less and less acceptable. In the light of this trend it behooves the manager who uses rage and personal tyranny as a system of motivating others into action to have a serious look at himself and his techniques of management.

15

How to Conduct
a Personal Inspection

"In life—as in bridge—one peek is worth two finesses."—ANON.

One of the neglected arts of management is that of *looking* at the situation. Very few courses at Harvard, Northwestern, Michigan, or California have anything to offer in regard to this vital skill of the manager. Yet, there's nothing that creates more social distance between a manager and his people than too much desk leadership at the expense of personal visitations and inspections.

The reasons for the chair-bound manager holding his pants to his chair are very persuasive. For one thing his in-basket seems to burgeon every time he gets away from the office. For another, he always seems to find a stack of 'phone messages awaiting him when he returns. Even more persuasive is the fact that if he doesn't go to people they seem to find their way to him, and he gains the feeling that he is keeping fully abreast of what is going on in the shop or field without making such visits. This is, of course, a false and misleading illusion, and one which can be extremely costly if continued over a period of time.

Getting out for a look at the actual scene of operations can sharpen the quality of decisions made in the office considerably. It provides a feel for local conditions. More importantly, it adds to his management decisions a generally higher quality in the mind of the person affected because they have the touch and aura of reality which chair-bound decisions seem to lack. There are, furthermore, some things which can only be judged from personal inspections. Housekeeping is but one of these. Let's look at the housekeeping example. Here's what one president says about plant tours he conducts:

> I know darn well they clean up special when I'm coming, but this doesn't dismay me. I know from inspecting the place whether or not the manager of the plant has sufficient control over operations to be able to enforce a special program upon demand if he is able to pull a good clean-up program on short notice.

Here's what a vice president of manufacturing says about inspections:

> I always attach a lot of importance to my trips, even though the only real things that are evident are housekeeping. If I go into a plant where everything is neat and orderly I have an impression that the place is under control. It may be possible that a plant looks like a pig-pen and actually runs like a clock, but my experience is just the opposite. If the manager can't control the things I can see with my eye on a brief visit, he probably has a lot of other things that are more basic that he's let slip too.

As with housekeeping, there are many things which can be awry that will never be reported. No plant manager ever walks into the boss's office and reports, "Our plant looks terrible." It takes an inspection by the boss to find out just how poor things are. Some other areas of the business which can best be observed from close-up inspection include maintenance of plant and equipment, the general tenor of work and pace of the work force, evidences of unsafe practice, the care of materials, and the general attitudes of people at work.

In addition to seeing what is going on, the manager *is seen* on his inspection trips, and this is an important facet of management and morale. The concept of the absentee boss is one which has great capacity to rile workers and managers alike.

Charles Bell, president of General Mills, Inc., insists that his executives spend much of their time out of the office visiting plants and sales districts. Beyond this he spends much of his own executive time out in the field as well. In addition, his board of directors change the location of their board meetings from place to place to be able to include plant tours in various plant locations as part of their agenda. Going even further, the company also holds unique "regional stockholder's meetings" in various parts of the country where the company operates, in order that the owners may see the properties which they hold on paper.

Yet, a visit in itself can be either good or bad. There are some methods of making such visits most effective that have worked well for managers, and some things to avoid as well.

Watching For the Important Things on a Visit

The experienced executive learns what to look for on a visit. Since he's probably going to be there only a few days or hours he can't hope to learn everything, and see everything that could be seen. This requires that he develop a sharp sense of rooting out the vital things to look for, and using them as indicators of the things he hasn't time to observe.

Plant and operating people have a vast facility for picking up which items the "old man" is going to inspect and making certain that they will be correct before his arrival. Yet, where this surface polish is all that has been applied, the smart inspector will pry into the basic operations very quickly to find the things swept under the rug. Four general areas seem to be productive in sorting out the important facts from the trivial about a plant or office.

1. *Do the people who are supposed to know have the answers?* Usually the plant or branch office tour is accompanied by the man or men in charge of the operation. The visitation can also be the occasion for a quiet but systematic quiz of the local boss, using items and events as they occur to provoke answers.

"How much scrap do we get from these machines?" or, "What's the grievance rate been in the foundry?" might be asked as these facilities are being inspected or viewed on the visit. The fact that the local manager doesn't know may not be damaging, but it's worth further investigation when he tells his boss he is ignorant of some local situation in too many instances. You might even do as Eugene MacNeice of Johnson and Johnson reported as his method of conducting such quizzes. MacNeice set up a point scoring system. It went something like this:

> "4"—if the man had the answer immediately and it was correct.
>
> "3"—if he said, "I don't know but will find out," then reported back with the correct answer shortly.
>
> "2"—if the man was very slow in reporting back with the facts (for example, more than two or three days).
>
> "1"—if the man had to be reminded to get the facts and report.
>
> "0"—if he failed to report even after reminder, or if he reported back incorrect facts.

This rating systm wasn't perfect, but it became a guide as to who was on top of the job and who wasn't when a long series of such scores were accumulated. MacNeice found that his best men consistently scored threes and fours, and his problem managers racked up zeroes or ones.

2. *Are the easily controllable things under control?* In every operation there are certain parts of the job which are easily controlled by the manager who is abreast of things in his area. In some plants this is housekeeping, and sloppiness is evidence of lack of discipline and control over the actions of employees. The only alternative here is the assumption that the manager likes to have the place unkempt. One manager puts it this way:

> It might be that a plant with unpainted machines and disorder and confusion in stock, machine parts and workplaces is underneath it a smoothly functioning machine, but most jalopies look like it, and most Cadillacs not only outrun the rattletrap, but they *look* as if they could.

This isn't to say that a foundry should look like a surgical manufacturer, but there are orderly foundries and sloppy ones. Nor are special periods of rush orders and extraordinary crises apt to find the place as neat as when a clean-up has just taken place. Putting these exceptional circumstances aside, however, housekeeping is one evidence of lack of control. Great stacks of rework product, a high accident frequency and severity rate, workers walking about in obvious violation of known safety rules, and gross evidences (or less obvious evidences) of carelessness and inattention can be danger signs that some of the controllable things aren't under firm control. At this point the inspector can begin to turn his attention to the management of the place.

3. *Is the surface representative of what lies beneath?* Inspections can be a terrific waste of time, and moreover be deceptive in some cases. Where an inspection seems to indicate that all is in order, but the quick view isn't representative of what's actually occurring, a false optimism and dangerous sense of security can come about. Probing beneath the surface in one or two instances can sometimes unearth any evidences of "glossing over" of poor conditions. Here's how one general manager does it:

> I use a system of one-two inspections as I make my tour. I may pull a sample of something here and there, a product off the line; or a chat with a worker. If everything seems to be OK on the basis of the first check I go along and look at the next thing. If I discover something wrong however, I stop and take a second look, and then maybe a third. Finally I'll probe just as deep as I need to to find out how bad things are. It's that first sample that triggers a deeper look however. It works surprisingly well.

4. *Does the inspection check out with other facts?* Before going on a plant-or-local-office tour it's a wise plan to get some basic facts about the place before leaving. Some of the figures might include labor relations, morale, cost accounting, spoilage, and so on. If something is showing up

very good or very bad in these figures, this is a hint as to where to look. High direct labor cost ought to be borne out with inspection evidence that lines are shut down or delayed. When you have a report that morale is great in the plant, but every employee you talk to seems disgruntled, it might be worth further investigation. The figures should merely be a guide to suggest places to visit and inspect personally. If the figures and the local inspection don't tally, this discrepancy should be followed up and clarified.

Showmanship in Personal Visits

One of the values in inspections is the opportunity it provides people working in the outside location to see the boss. This is important to them since it gives them a chance to personally size up the caliber of top management in their company. It would be a drastic mistake to assume that because they aren't all staring directly at the visitor during the visit, that they aren't seeing everything that goes on. This means that the boss as well as the people and the plant are on display, and should be governed accordingly.

The first and most obvious requirement is that dignity, friendliness and cordiality be the rule of the day. This doesn't mean one must be a hail-fellow or a back slapper, but means that reactions are positive when you see things you like. If things seem to be okay and management is satisfied with what it finds on such visits, it's sound strategy to express this satisfaction to the employees or in their hearing. It also means a willingness to try to remember faces and names between visits, and to recall past associations, even temporary ones. Here's how failure to do so can affect relationships adversely:

> "I've met our vice president five times now," a mechanic reported in a metal factory, "and each time I had to be introduced again, and I'm sure he didn't know who I was any of the last four times. You'd think he wouldn't be so dumb as to forget."

Admittedly this vice president met many hundreds of people each year, and could possibly forget. It actually proved to be a habit in which the vice president never tried to remember anybody's name, even those whom he saw daily. This coldness toward interpersonal contacts reflects itself in employee attitudes quickly. It's possible that such people might do better to avoid visits entirely since they do more harm than good.

How much time should an executive spend with an individual employee? Chris Argyris of Yale, who analysed many such visits, reports that the average successful chat with an employee can run around ninety seconds, and during that time the benefits of personal contact and showmanship can be achieved. A simple question oriented toward the employee, not critical in tone nor intent, and rewarded with an evidence of interest and a sincere thanks for the information is sound visitation and inspection strategy.

Personal attire is part of the showmanship of an inspection where the objective is as much to be seen as to see the plant. When the executive is visiting the plant and is on display, he should look like an executive. If the mores of the front office are that he can wear colorful vests and separates in trousers and jacket, perhaps this might be set aside for the visit. Neat and quietly expensive clothes are probably the safest as a rule. Hand painted neckties, yodel hats with shaving brushes in the band and the like have been found to bring out the derision latent in employee views of managers from afar. He should of course always follow the rules of the shop in regard to hard hats, safety glasses, coveralls and the like if they are part of the pattern in the shop. Most safety rules are considered by employees as originating in the president's office if not higher, and for an executive to violate them leaves a bad taste in their mouths, and undermines the local manager in his safety efforts.

A sound briefing on the big problems facing the people in the local office or plant is sound strategy. This provides the visiting inspector a chance to ask some intelligent questions which indicates that he's at least interested enough in their affairs to inquire and get informed about the plant. Probably the use of this information can be limited to stopping by the machine of the employee operating an important job on crucial operation and saying:

"Hello Bill, I thought I'd drop around and see how you're making out on this job. As you know, we consider it one of the hottest in the company, and I thought I'd see how it was going."

The Ethics of Making Inspections

One of the reasons that many managers refuse to make inspections is the resistance they occasionally get from lower level management over their too frequent inspections. There's some sound reasoning behind this resistance. Most of the reasoning grows out of the fact that all too often top management people don't observe the unwritten rules of the game in inspections and visitations. These rules go as follows:

1. *Don't undercut the management on the spot.* It's a cheap appeal for

popularity in the eyes of foremen and first line management for the executive to visit the plant and water down the first line supervisors' authority through dealing directly with employees. The employee who has nerve and brass may use his contacts with the top man to work his points, and settle an argument which he's been losing with his foreman, by going over his head. If he can do this with the tacit consent—or even the invitation —of the top man, he's "used" the top man by whipsawing him against his immediate boss.

2. *Always build the status of local management.* Unless things are so horribly fouled up that the local manager is about to be relieved on the spot—even then it should be done privately—visitations and inspections should be used to enhance his importance in the eyes of his employees. State how much confidence you have in local management, and imply that he has close contact, communication and confidence of the top.

3. *Find fault privately.* If things which aren't up to snuff are discovered, it's perfectly acceptable to ask questions, but the hostile, directive, or interrogatory question that puts the local manager on the spot before his subordinates should be reserved for later. If several layers of supervision are between the visiting fireman and the local manager they should be on hand, and all criticism should be routed through them.

4. *Don't generalize on too scanty evidence.* Take the case of the president who visited a plant and found a man reading a racing form in the maintenance office. He immediately walked up to the man and ordered him to put the "damned paper in the wastebasket and get to work." Imagine his chagrin when the man coolly informed him that he was an outside telephone repairman who was waiting for his partner to come back with some parts from the truck, and furthermore since he didn't work for that company but the phone company the executive could go off into a corner and soak his head. Naturally this story spread like wildfire around the plant and the whole company. The Old Man might better have identified his target before letting loose his heaviest guns.

While this instance was merely one of foolishness on the part of the executive, more damaging circumstances are those where a visiting inspector generalizes upon half the facts about his own people.

> Take the case of the visiting auditor who was touring a regional warehouse for an auto supply firm. As he was walking through the yard he saw a workman burning trash and noticed that several tires were among the items being destroyed. In his report back at the office he reported that the warehouse manager was burning tires— no explanation, just that they were burning tires. Naturally an explanation was asked for by letter. The local manager was furious at

the implication that he would destroy good tires, or even recappable ones. The tires, he explained in a hot letter in return, were completely unrepairable and had been taken in trade-in and his procedures followed company policy exactly. He further went on to complain bitterly about "spies and snoopers" who would see such things and not report them to him before going back to company headquarters to write snide letters.

This leads us to the next rule of ethics for inspection tours.

5. *Let the local man explain his side.* When the inspecting executive sees things which he thinks might be wrong his first step is to ask the local manager in charge to tell him why a certain thing is being done. "I don't understand why you are doing this..." is a good preface to bringing up such situations. The act of putting people on the defensive in the face of what seems to be damning evidence, in itself causes all inspections to be viewed with a jaundiced eye. Even when he has a chance to explain, when it is done under the circumstances of being in the trial court, it has numerous bad effects. When he is accosted by such things as, "I notice that you are doing such and such a thing, and it would seem to me that you are making a mistake," it makes any explanation which follows an alibi rather than a reason, and the fact of being placed in such a position by the inspecting executive is the basis for resentment. In most cases local conditions have created reasons why procedures have been developed. Asking for these facts and feelings first may make the whole thing seem plausible. If it does not, the executive should then move firmly into explaining the reasons why it must be changed.

How To Detect Cover-Ups During Inspections

The inspection process itself can have the harmful effect of giving the inspector a false sense of well-being and security where he glosses over the underlying facts. This is especially true of such matters as morale and general attitudes of employees.

> In one steel company the president toured a mill and among other things inquired of the superintendents how they would evaluate the morale in the plant. Either because they didn't really know or because they wanted to present a favorable front, they all reported that things were normal. Later that day the evening shift pulled a wild-cat walkout which was followed by the other shifts following suit.

How can a visiting executive determine whether or not things are not what they seem to be, and when he is getting accurate information? This becomes especially difficult when he must skirt around his assigned officials to get this information. Here are some guides to getting at these things:

1. *He can talk to people.* An integral part of many visits should be informal chats with people at all levels. In addition to making small talk and complimenting outstanding people (suggestion award winners, for example) he can ask such questions as these:

> What is your job here? How long have you worked here?
> How do you like your job? Why?
> What don't you like? Why?
> What could we do to make your job easier, safer, better?

Asked in casual but direct fashion, these questions can produce factual information which indicates feelings and opinions of people and from which generalizations about morale and loyalty to the organization can be the basis of general appraisal of the condition there.

2. *Comparisons with other locations.* Standards of performance for the organization can be carried from one plant to another by the inspector who has seen many such plants in operation. He notes that the housekeeping in one plant is better than another, or that one plant has more people on certain jobs than another. These are evidences which should lead to follow up and closer examination.

> The manufacturing manager for a can plant with national distribution has a habit of reading production figures from feeder counters at the end of the line as he tours the plants, especially on key lines. Although he probably has a general acquaintance with differences in output, the fact that he sees a figure which seems low to him can open the door for such questions as:
> "I notice you've only made 10,000 containers on this line today, and if my memory is correct we should be getting fifteen for this line at this time. What seems to be the problem here?"
> He reports that this often opens the door to general discussions on what's wrong with maintenance in the plant, the training of operators, relations with the sales department, or the effectiveness of production scheduling against the machines.

The purpose in probing into such specific things isn't to investigate the single instance of low production, but to open the door to more generalized discussions of plant operations with the management. In one plant he found that the fault was his own, for he had vetoed a mechanical overhaul program several months before, and it was having serious effects on direct labor costs in that plant. Getting effective use out of such comparisons can only be done by the person with knowledge of many plants and ability to recall accurately the standards and actual performance from plant to plant.

In one large drug firm where the manufacturing head sees that one plant is way ahead of another in housekeeping, morale, or maintenance of equipment he suggests that the manager of the less effective plant visit one of the better managed ones and "pick up a few ideas." This ordinarily has a sound effect of stimulating the lesser man, at the same time it improves his ability to change things through exposing him to sounder practices that have worked.

3. *Have some information in advance.* One of the ways in which inspections can be probing in nature is to go armed with facts and figures which need some investigation. If, for example, a morale or opinion survey has been taken recently, these results can be the basis for focussing attention during the inspection on visible causes of difficulty. In more cases than one might suspect, the tangible effects of bad conditions can be visibly seen and checked by inspection, and with the local flavor in hand some genuine assistance and counsel in means of improvement can be made. Working from the accounting report, the morale audit, the down time report can be ephemeral and theoretical. The principal use of such information comes in actually using it to effect improvements. This ordinarily requires some personal looks at the scene as well as generalization and solutions based upon pure logic developed in a corporate headquarters.

The Case for the Leader Being Seen

There are few instances in management where the personal qualities of the leader have greater impact upon the organization than during a personal visit. Throughout history the leader of great movements, the general, the statesman, the monarch, the president who was able to lead the great organization to excel was the man who had the capacity for being seen favorably by large numbers of his followers.

Modern psychology has largely ignored this factor in leadership, despite the formidable array of evidence of its importance. The leader who appears often before his men can transmit enthusiasm, sincerity, and zeal in his people where he manages these things effectively. It is one of the most obvious places where the physical bearing and manner of the leader has significance. His personality traits become crystallized and summed up in his manner during the ninety second exposure.

Nobody has studied extensively the importance of appearance in a leader, yet in personal leadership of large groups of people close attention to this facet of managerial ability is a key that unlocks many doors, and offsets inability to deliver speeches that bristle with intellectual qualities.

In all of our attention to the qualities of management, and the skills of the manager in organizing, planning, controlling, and deskmanship, we have often overlooked the necessity of personal appearances before large groups of subordinates as a vital factor. Obviously dynamic or showy qualities in visits can't offset sloppy staff work, or make up for a chaotic organization plan. Yet, it can unite the people behind their top leaders as few other procedures can do.

Many of the techniques of modern management of people are designed to allay the evils which come from failure to inspect and visit the scene where the goods are sold or made. Appraisal systems, budgetary controls, and similar logical procedures all too often owe their existence to a desire on the part of top men to remain apart from their subordinates. Inspection and personal leadership are due for a revival.

What are the occasions when inspections and visits should take place? One of the most obvious is at events where people are gathered for some honor-giving occasion. The safety award dinner, the annual foreman's banquet, the suggestion award, the sales training meeting, or the management development session are all good excuses which should not be missed. It affords a means of making a personal impact by the top man who has arrived because of the very leadership qualities which would make such inspections and visits to the field or plant bring the greatest return in action and results from the organization.

Part III

PERSONAL TECHNIQUES FOR ACTION-GETTING MANAGEMENT

"This body of ours is something like an electric battery in which a mysterious power latently lies. When this power is not properly brought into operation it either grows mouldy and withers away or is warped and expresses itself abnormally."

—D. T. SUZUKI

16

Harnessing Aggressiveness
in Management

"The rung of a ladder was never meant to rest upon, but only to hold a man's foot long enough to enable him to put the other somewhat higher."

—Thomas Huxley

Aggressiveness ranks high among the qualities sought in managers. Every company is looking for self-starting young men who can show initiative and follow-through.

But the overly aggressive person arouses resistance. Others will go out of their way to block his progress.

For this reason, top executives declare, they spend much of their time doing two things:

1. Trying to stimulate subordinates who don't show enough aggressiveness.

2. Trying to straighten out those who let aggressiveness get the best of them.

Methods of attaining the first objective—salary increases, fringe benefits, status symbols—are generally understood and applied. But how to put brakes on aggressiveness, once it gets out of hand, is more complex and harder to manage.

It is not impossible, however, once we recognize the motives that lead to aggressiveness and the personality changes that show it is becoming a handicap.

A number of studies show that, although other motives may exist, those that drive a man to accomplishment are primarily three:

- A desire for power.
- A desire for a good reputation.
- A desire for wealth.

Let's look a these motives and at the danger points in each. In every case we will find a stage where caution is indicated. If this stage is recognized, the still effects of having too much of a good thing can be prevented.

The Desire for Mastery

Deep inside nearly every successful man is an intense desire to be best. He might want to be the number one production man in the organization. His every action is calculated to carry him toward that. Naturally, this requires that he acquire some skills in outwitting his competitors or, more often, outworking them. There are six stages of this desire to be top dog.

The first stage is the highly-sought-after desire to excel in his chosen field. He has such a sense of craftsmanship and pride in his work that he simply won't turn out an inferior job nor will he be bested in quantity of output. This is the basic building block by which most managers and employees achieve mastery of their field. One of the great problems of modern management is to develop more tools and skills for instilling this desire in more people.

Usually this desire to excel propels a man quickly into the next stage. Here he becomes the joy of his boss, because he demonstrates that he has a self-development habit that leads him to acquire new skills as well as to do effectively the things he already knows. He studies his own past efforts, corrects his own mistakes, and learns how to repeat his successes in new situations.

In the third stage he raises his eyes to see how the other fellow is doing. Rather than working to meet some personal standard, he tends to increase his efforts and performance to exceed the best efforts of his best competitors. He gets real enjoyment out of rivalry with other good men. He especially enjoys winning against tough opposition.

The next stage involves his emotions and his ego in his work to a degree which wasn't previously apparent. When he faces a tough competitive situation he learns to stretch himself to win, and develops the capacity of working at paces that he himself didn't know he could maintain.

In these first four stages we see an ideal manager for a modern company.

Every incentive we provide leads him to develop winning skills, and use them best when the chips are down.

The danger point comes in the fifth and sixth stages where he begins to blow his top when he's frustrated in his drive for mastery.

In these last two stages basically sound drives have turned into belligerence and hostility. In its mildest form this crops up as maliciousness and nagging. At worst it appears as temper tantrums.

A hothead can add a touch of drive and energy to the management team, but sometimes at a cost which the company can't afford. A midwestern banker learned this. He hired an aggressive man to head his new-business development. Blessed with a keen sense of competition, he shortly began to go after, and get, the taken-for-granted customers of other banks. His attitude was one of open competition for customers. For a while his own bank president was delighted. Then one day, a customer decided to withdraw his account. The new man made a hard sales pitch. The customer, also hotheaded, gave him some sales resistance. Soon they were out in the parking lot behind the bank swinging at each other. Police intervened before damage was done to anything except the bank's prestige.

This is an extreme case, but uncontrolled temper can constitute a problem for the manager who tries to build a hard-hitting team of aggressive people.

The too-aggressive person often develops a general attitude that other people are inferior or no good. This puts a limit on where he can be assigned, because subordinates and associates quickly sense such an attitude.

Such a man will surround himself with compliant people, since only passive personalities can stand being around him long. His reactions to opposition are usually painful, not only to the objects of his wrath, but to those who deserve it. Such men are quick to fire people: a loyal subordinate who thinks for himself, or an advertising agency which doesn't agree with his whims.

In the final stage, such a man becomes clearly revealed, his inhibitions stripped away, and his infantilism exposed.

Three Cures for Excessive Desire for Mastery

How do you help an angry man control his wrath and channel it into useful lines?

1. Most men learn it by feeling the hard knocks which others give them when they behave that way. Letting him get the cold shoulder from

colleagues, or being left out of the social niceties of the work group, is one way. Anger as a system of obtaining mastery is a self-feeding device. If it works once it will be tried again. If it produces only hard knocks or slapped wrists, it will be used with more reluctance.

2. A knuckle-rapping by the boss can be equally effective if done early.

3. For the fellow who has an advanced case which is causing over-all output and quality to suffer, there's no cure, unless the man himself recognizes his condition and tries to control it. Normally his superior can point out that his work and personal progress are being adversely affected by his tantrums, and can seek agreement that the condition exists and needs improvement. This is often slow work and occasional lapses are to be expected, coupled with some guilt afterwards. Failing this, the superior might seek professional advice to advantage.

In one case, a competent young manager of sales for a large company was suffering from a bad case of egotism. His records in selling were excellent. Not stopping there, this aggressive fellow undertook to tell manufacturing, engineering, and just about everyone else about their shortcomings.

Not wanting to lose his excellent abilities, but pressed for action by his subordinates, the general manager rotated him into a position as plant manager. After two months of trying to apply some of his methods there he asked to be sent back to sales, a chastened and wiser man.

The factory wasn't hurt too badly because the professionals at the next lower level had kept things going in spite of him. They had also contributed greatly to his growing-up processes by pointing out the effects of his impulsive and ill-formed decisions. Not everyone can have such valuable and quick training, but the principle is sound. An unjustified feeling of mastery can be brought into line by putting the man in a spot where he can taste failure.

Desire for a Good Reputation

Every man on the rise learns quickly the value of a good reputation, and quietly works to establish one for himself, since it's obviously one way of getting where he wants to go.

The realization that reputation is valuable comes when a man is noticed and possibly praised for doing good work. More important than the praise, however, to the aggressive man is the fact that now he becomes a candidate for jobs further up the ladder.

"The first time I really began to feel that I might make the grade in this company was when I heard that two managers were squabbling over who was going to get me for a vacancy in his division."

That's a statement by a company president looking back upon his career. The realization that a reputation is an extension of the good work you've done is a key phase in reputation-building. Soon the aggressive and competent man finds that he is in a position to select the spot he'll move to.

As one general manager put it:

"At one time, after five years out of college, four different executives asked that I be assigned to their departments. I sized up the situation and applied for the job with a small division which was growing fast and needed somebody who could do a job. It was the smartest thing I ever did. I rode with that division until I was the only logical candidate to be general manager."

Having arrived in a position where he's now a proven man, the manager develops his own opportunities and creates his own reputation-building opportunities. Here's how one such manager did it:

"When I first took over the X division I sized things up carefully, and asked myself, 'What's the tallest weed that I can chop down here?' The answer was in manufacturing costs, and this was where my experience lay. I mapped out a cost-reduction program that trimmed away the fat left and right. Naturally, the profit of the division improved considerably and I was tabbed as a profit-maker. This paved the way for assignment to the Y division, the biggest one in the company."

All this is desirable and should be cultivated in a manager. It is when we get to the next stage that the first symptoms of danger begin to appear.

At this stage our man has built up supreme confidence in his ability to lick most of the problems he may face. The confidence sometimes extends to other things about which he has little real competence, but which he is willing to assume are just as easy of solution.

When he makes speeches he talks confidently about foreign relations, politics, or women's hats. In its most harmless form this sometimes reflects itself in a newly acquired expertness in the manners and fashions of successful people. Because he's successful, he uses money effectively to establish an air of distinction and superiority. He's likely at this point to become an authority on fine arts, good food, fine fittings, good cigars, and other accoutrements of success.

All of this may even he helpful, since it gives him color which can cause others to have confidence in him.

It's when he goes beyond this into the sixth stage that he is likely to have trouble—along with the company which employs him. At this stage he's out of touch with reality, and only hears the things that agree with his preconceptions. He loses his skill in listening to others, especially those below him in rank, assuming that he needn't hear the whole story to see the basic nugget of truth. He becomes immune to criticism and irritable when he hears it.

As this attitude hardens, he becomes less tolerant of opposition, considering it impudent. Here's how one such man's subordinate described him:

"Nobody dares to tell him the truth if it's against his opinion, and everybody tries to guess what he wants to hear before opening his mouth. He can destroy months of work with a single snort."

When such a person takes a fall, as he almost always does, he'll resort to tricks to feed his ego. He deceives himself first, becomes more skilled in alibis, and avoids hard tests of his skills in order to avoid further failures, however small. If facts get in the way he'll duck them. If his predictions fall short of reality, he'll question reality rather than his own judgment.

What to Do When Desire for Reputation Leads to Excess Vanity

Once a manager has gone beyond the danger point in building a reputation, there's still some hope for salvaging him. The guide for solution of the vanity problem (which is what passing the danger point creates) lies in prevention, rather than cure.

Here are some steps in prevention and cure:

1. Every young man on the rise should be coached in the techniques of reputation-building by a boss who still holds his future in his hands. This may be done by his own manager, or by a management development counselor, if necessary.

"One method I've used to show young fellows on the way up how to avoid getting a swelled head is to point to some examples that are commonly known in the company or outside," one counselor states.

2. Several training courses for managers are therapy-centered and attempt to hold up a mirror for such men to see themselves. Commonly known as "sensitivity training," these courses have done wonders in helping people see themselves.

3. Occasionally a survey of employee opinion will reflect images of

top management. Such results seldom cut through the hard shell of a tough case, but in some instances they startle the fellow who has recently fallen into this pattern.

In one company, a general survey of management practices included the question, "How do you see your boss?" and gave the subordinates an opportunity to check one of several frank answers. The result was that the boss did a sharp reversal on his practice of not listening, squelching ideas, and treating subordinates like dolts.

4. The company's management-appraisal system permits a man and his boss to sit down together and talk frankly about such problems as this. The limitation here lies in the incapability of the average line manager when it comes to dealing with complex personality counseling.

One large food company's appraisal procedure provides that the content of such talks be limited purely to the subordinate's performance. If performance is bad, then the reasons become legitimate items for frank discussion. If the reasons lie in the vanity and unwillingness of the man to listen, then this is discussed as a part of his performance. The theory is that, unless a habit or trait has affected performance, it's none of the company's business.

5. A man's peers are the best people to tell him his problem in instances where he is too high up the ladder to be treated by normal methods.

The executive vice president of one company was suffering from a severe case of inflated ego. One of his subordinates convinced him that he should attend a management course.

After trying some of his tactics on his classmates there, all of whom were just as important in their companies as he was in his own, he caught the idea. On the last day of the course he asked permission to address the class.

"I'd like to apologize," he said, "for being the insufferable fathead that you saw when I came here. I'd like also to thank you for the kindly fashion in which you took me down a peg or two. I think this has been the most valuable experience in my business career."

Another executive was asked to serve as chairman of a volunteer community chest drive in his city. His insufferable vanity shortly got him into trouble. Finally, several executives who were also working on the drive cornered him and told him some things about himself. He saw the whole drive threatened with collapse unless he tempered his ego, and began to listen to others. The experience had substantial carryover on his behavior in his own company.

The Desire for Wealth

In picking a man who is likely to maintain a steady drive for the top, it's sound strategy to choose one who wants better things than he has now. These goals may be luxury cars, a bigger house, money in the bank, a fat stock portfolio, or to send his children to a fashionable college. The cash for better things is a strong motivator. Men go through definite stages in satisfying their desire for material success.

In the early stages, the young manager makes up his mind that he wants a higher standard of living and decides to get it by working harder and smarter.

The next stage comes when he gets many of the things that he associates with a better standard of living but discovers that he can probably do even better.

"When I was foreman in the plant, I decided that we would some day live in one of the nice old houses on Main Street," one executive said. "When I became assistant manager, we made it. After we'd lived there a while we began to eye one of the bigger houses up on the hill. That was a big turning point in my career. I began to figure out a five-year plan for moving into the plant manager's job, and I made that, too."

The next stage comes when he has achieved most of the outward symbols of success and can afford most of the dreams he had as a young man. At this point he either levels off or sets his sights on gaining the big successes. The new goal may become an estate and financial independence, or he may begin to eye the cruisers at the boat show with a new interest, or maintain two houses, one at the lake and one in town. He may start talking to architects about that dream house in the fashionable part of an exclusive suburb. He finds that managing his personal affairs is a fair-sized business problem in itself. Here's how one executive put it:

"I found that owning a house in a community with the inherited-money boys was heady stuff. I got an old farm, modernized it, bought six Aberdeen Angus steers, and joined a country club."

This step occasionally leads the ambitious manager into the dangerous fourth stage. This is where he begins to discount against the income he expects from his next promotion. He stretches his standard of living too far, neglects his estate-planning, and lets spending exceed income. Often he finds that his expense account is keeping him going, and he treats it with a liberality which is just short of outrageous.

The family budget is a thing of the past. The tension and strain of maintaining living standards which are beyond his income result in some tension in the job which may have the beneficial effect of driving him to terrific levels of output. The truth is that most people who get into this position carry it off. An unhappy few stumble and fall. It takes strong nerves.

One executive search consultant reports:

"I always consider it in my favor if the man we are trying to hire away from his present company is living beyond his income. This means he'll likely listen to our offer if it means a boost of that eight to ten thousand dollars which he thinks will solve his problems. Usually the money won't help."

The final stage comes when his financial woes catch up with him. One sales executive was taken off a traveling job where his expense account was high and put in an office job. This caught him in a financial bind and he wound up in a trap he couldn't handle. The company spent huge sums bailing him out. He finally quit. Financial problems growing out of overextension are frequent. When they occur they create company problems.

The Cure for Too Much Desire for Worldly Success

As with many serious ailments, an ounce of prevention is worth a pound of therapy. One executive describes his method like this:

"Whenever I can, I talk to the younger fellows about their personal estate-building program, and try to get them on a long-range plan that includes savings, insurance, a retirement plan, annuities, and a sound real-estate plan."

Many companies offer special programs which advise their younger executives on estate-building, and make counselors available at no cost.

An oil company holds periodic meetings of its executives to which the wives are invited.

While the husbands are off talking sales or refining, the wives are attending discussion groups led by a professor who talks about how the wife can help the husband succeed—and especially on financial management.

Other companies try to prepare their people through adroit planning of the compensation and benefit plans which they provide executives. This is coupled with a management newsletter which includes some professional and down-to-earth advice on personal-affairs planning for executives.

One insurance company requires executives to file annual statements

of their financial condition. Those in hot water—or on the verge of it—
are told bluntly to get things in line.

In a large midwestern bank, the senior vice presidents are held responsible for the private financial affairs of the younger men reporting to them.
If on begins to live beyond what seems to be normal for his income, he
is invited to explain.

Drastic as these steps seem for most companies, there is still room for
informal chats on performance which slide smoothly into more personal
aspects of finance and personal estate-planning.

Under such a plan, the executive can appraise how eager the subordinate has become for worldly goods and, from his own experience, drop
broad hints about curbing what appears to be undue emphasis on outward
evidences of success. The latter would appear to be most workable for
the average company.

17

How to Be a Lucky Executive

"Fortune is the ruler of half of our actions, but she allows the other half or thereabouts to be ruled by us."

—NICCOLO MACHIAVELLI

Survey the average corporate employee and he'll tell you that the reason he's not further along, or the reason the top manager is where he is, is because the successful were smiled upon by lady luck. The concept of luck is a vast face-saving device for many of us, for it prevents us from having to confront our own personal shortcomings and inadequacies. The best part of this entire system of reasoning is that there is an element of truth which can be demonstrated regularly. Pure chance, and blind luck exist and affect the course of companies and the careers of people. They also provide a wonderful excuse for failure, a rationale for not working hard and an alibi for poor performance.

While it's probably impossible for an executive to eliminate luck there are ways which he can put it to use in his competitive plans, and can become a "lucky" executive and make his company one of the "lucky" few which succeed and grow. There's no disagreeing that luck is a factor in success and company growth. Even the august Stanford Research Institute lists *luck* as one of the factors which has characterized growth companies along with identification and orientation to growth fields, willingness to drop dying lines, courageous and energetic management, and so on.

One of the persuasive arguments for *luck* as a factor in management success is the lack of uniformity in management practices which brought success to one organization and disaster to another. One firm follows all the textbook rules of management in such things as organizing, planning, controlling, motivating, and developing people. It would be a joy to the case writer from the university School of Business Administration. Yet it staggers along with mediocre growth and profit while another without a bit of attention to these things coins vast profits and grows at an exponential rate. In another instance one company follows certain practices and loses money, where its competitor follows the same rules and makes great sums. In still a third instance two firms follow entirely different approaches to management practice and end up equally profitable and successful. These three instances would make a good case for the presence of luck and its significance as a cause of failure or success of a business and its management. Yet, to impute the differences to luck alone would be to oversimplify. What are some rules which can put luck on the side of an executive and prevent it going against him? The basic rule is a simple one:

> *Luck shows its power in business where there has been no provision to resist that power as it appears.*

Applying this rule consistently and through large and small decisions can improve the odds with which one deals with the phenomena of luck, and increases the chances of its being "good" instead of "bad" luck. Let's take an example:

> Johnson and Johnson in its controller's department has a group known as the "profits committee." In the early part of each year the profits committee meets with the management committee to review forecasted operations. Throughout the year it periodically reviews performance against forecast. These provide the basis for switching efforts and resources if one area falls down and overall profits are threatened by "bad luck" in one product or market line, and to capitalize on "good luck" in another.

Our point here isn't one of financial management, but the control of fortunes and changes in luck as they appear through making provision for bad effects before they actually occur. The manager who makes things happen is more than a full-back who charges full tilt into lines of opposition. He also provides for safeguards against the ruin which can come through changes in circumstances beyond his control. Blind trust in luck can bring about ruin if the manager counts on luck alone to provide him favorable advantages. Control of luck means setting up barriers to contain the flood of bad luck when it runs high, and these defenses must be constructed during the periods when things are running smoothly.

This change in outside conditions which affect the business accounts for the differences in results which can come through different management methods. It likewise accounts for the success of one person and the failure of another where both use the same approach.

The lucky manager adopts every strategy to gain a superior position that can be protected against loss in the future. This superior position is comprised of many different features, and being lucky means knowing what these components of a superior position are, and when each should be used. Oswald Knauth, former treasurer of Macy's, identifies these things in the retail business as "trade advantages."

> One concern stresses its reliability or service, another its low prices, this one its wide selection, that one exclusiveness, and still another the style of its products. One newspaper will become distinguished for its wide coverage of news, another for its special features.

Such choice among alternative courses or policies of course demands a wide knowledge of trends.

Keeping Abreast of Latest Trends

The control of luck, and of being prepared for competition, means that the executive identifies the trends and conditions which must be controlled to prevent great losses from reversal in fortune. What are some of these areas in which he must keep his flanks covered to offset the possibility of "bad luck" overtaking him?

1. *Know-how.* Through research and development, and through training he must keep his firm ahead of the competitor—domestic or foreign—who can smash into his market armed with new know-how and put him at a disadvantage.

2. *Changes in taste.* Consumer tastes are fickle and you may find the firm which is too greatly wedded to one style or one model left in the lurch. Annual model changes in automobiles demand that careful attention be paid to predicting styling changes in several years in advance, for example.

3. *Trends in location.* Not only do markets change—from the city to suburbia, for example—but availability of low cost labor, and closeness to raw materials may be important. Weston Instruments moved many of its meter-manufacturing operations to Puerto Rico in the early fifties to take advantage of lower labor costs and favorable governmental assistance to meet competition from European and Asian countries, thus forestalling competition from abroad.

4. *Competitive products.* Established products may find themselves hard-pressed by new products which compete for the same markets with-

out being identical in kind, glass jars competing with tin cans, for instance. Offsetting the possible ill effects of such changes can be made through buttressing the product with services, quick delivery, easy replacement and parts, or other distribution and service advantages which the new product can't hope to provide.

5. *Trade connections.* The connection with a good supplier or distributor can help offset catastrophic effects of new products, or new processes entering the market where they must compete against such connections. Yet, trade connections wear out, and changes in distribution systems, consolidations of suppliers, and similar modifications of trade connections must be watched and allowed for constantly.

Other trends which may be equally important that have a direct bearing upon management luck and the supports which must be built to protect against "bad luck" include such things as:

> reputation of the firm for quality
> labor supply
> changes in labor leadership
> political climate
> changes in tariffs
> technological changes
> supplies of raw materials
> changes in wages and salaries
> particular manpower shortages (engineers, etc.)
> retirement or death of key executives
> price inflation
> price collapses
> price cutting by competitors
> new merchandising methods
> changes in government regulations

Let's look at some examples of how managers have faced up to bad luck that confronted them, and came through without damage where others failed.

> Dayton's department store in Minneapolis was faced with a possible decline of business in their downtown store through the construction of shopping centers in the outlying sections of the city. Rather than simply renting space in such a center it constructed one of the largest and most unusual shopping centers in the country in its Southdale center. Thus it not only met the competition of such centers, but actually assumed leadership through outdoing all other centers and drawing shoppers from all other shopping areas, not only to its own store, but to the other stores in the center who were its tenants.

Such provision for harmful changes can extend to the personal career planning of the manager as well. In one large utility the middle level of accounting supervisors were confronted with the problem of data processing equipment being installed and making many of their skills obsolete. One group in such a company requested the management to organize a study group to instruct them in electronics and machine accounting to put them abreast of these newest developments. Management eagerly complied, and not only trained them in programming, and the grammar of machine language, but also probed into possible future changes through courses in operations research and managerial economics which refurbished the skills of the men attending.

Predicting the Hot Item of the Future

Hard luck often takes a heavy toll in people who have continued doing things the same old way, busily occupied with their daily tasks, oblivious of the new things which are already on the horizon. Fortunately for most alert managers such new innovations are a long time in coming, and offer the vigilant a chance to foresee what will be ahead and to prepare for it. Generally there are four major ways in which a manager can keep abreast of what the important agenda items will be for him in the future (and for his company).

He can keep abreast of the current literature. Most management magazines today are keenly alert to anything new. The pressures of editorial deadlines, and the demand of the readers for current and new information requires that its writers and editors be more than simple reporters of the existing methods. The great pressure in the giant publishing houses is for new and novel things. Often these are researched and scouted out with great resourcefulness, and presented with clarity for the management reader. The amount of information about new and promising methods, techniques, and trends contained in these publications is a vital factor in management peeks into the future. As W. J. Arnold, management editor of *Business Week,* puts it:

> We're more interested in what's going to be common practice five years from now than we are in what is going on today—although we like to watch what the leaders and successful firms are doing right now too.

Still another source of information on the important topic of the future is the *management or trade association meeting.* Speakers here are selected for their experience in novel and pioneering practices. American Management Association, for example, prefers the company which has something new and interesting to the same old stories of ordinary practice.

Watching the leading companies is a likely source of ideas for the future. Every new idea finds its roots quickly in some large and already successful company. Such pace-setters as IBM, GE, Sears, United States Steel, and the Bell System often innovate in management methods and provide a useful guide to what the thinking manager should be watching with interest.

University business schools and social science departments often are the focal point for new ideas. Colleges of industrial engineering often generate new ideas that find their way into industrial practice. Seminars by such universities can provide the executive with some guides as to trends which he should watch.

In all four there is the assumption that the manager who would avoid bad luck occasionally gets out of the office and his own company and talks with other managers. From them he gets the feel of new items and how important they are apt to become. This can be extended to stating that he often gets out of his own town or region and visits national meetings where executives from all parts of the country are in attendance in order to avoid provincialism and inbreeding of ideas.

Planning for the Unexpected

Luck seems to fall hardest on firms when their executives were unprepared for a change.

> One large newspaper chain has a plan for dealing with shortages of newsprint, through an arrangement with an alternate supplier, and a mutual agreement for exchange of resources for limited periods during emergencies.

This preparation for emergencies, or unexpected catastrophies is never easy to lend a sense of urgency to (until the firm has been through one sad experience), but it's a basic to averting the effects of hard luck. W. Benton Harrison, vice president of finance for Sylvania Electric products, division of General Telephone Company, states that the key ingredient is a "long range frame of mind" for all managers. This frame of mind, he states, is based on:

- *Application:* Planning is work.
- *Study:* All angles must be taken into consideration.
- *Brainpower:* The qualitative aspects of planning should form a backstop for the quantitative to avoid misdirection of effort.

- *The will to plan:* If planning is a chore, the results will reflect the planner's poor attitude.
- *Communication:* Everyone in the organization must understand plans in order to cooperate in carrying them out.

Or take the economic planning and market research of RCA which is designed to offset the effect of chance and luck upon the future of this electronics giant. E. Dorsey Foster, their vice president of economic planning, outlines how his company does it. Long range planning is a vital activity in RCA, he states, because it "must be designed to provide a framework for the tactical guidance of existing operations, as well as to enable the company to develop entirely new concepts and areas of operation."

The underlying philosophy here isn't one of being defensive against the ravages of change and bad luck. It's more likely that it will bring bad luck to competitors who aren't as vigilant in planning the future and making provisions for changes. Company weakness, internal or in relation to competitive position, Dorsey states, may be spotted and exposed for correction. The capabilities of key personnel are highlighted, the necessity for providing sufficient depth of personnel and the uncovering of latent talent is brought out.

If there's a place where this logical process can break down, it's in the area of assumptions which must be made about the future. Every manager must have some clear ideas of where he thinks over-all economic trends are headed, and know why he thinks that way. Some of the areas where a manager must make such assumptions include:

- whether the cold war will continue
- whether high government expenditure will continue
- changes in composition of spending (from aircraft to missiles, etc.)
- rate of population growth
- growth patterns in basic industry (housing, autos, etc.)
- direction and rate of consumer buying power
- how effective research and development will be.

Manpower planning has an especially important role to play in preparing for the unexpected. A force of managers and professionals who are competent to deal with change is perhaps just as important in preparing for the unforeseen as any forward looking projection could possibly be. As one manager puts it:

> If I can build a strong flexible corps of managers at every level I won't worry about changes and unexpected occurrences because

they'll be equipped to handle them. If I don't have such people on my staff I'm licked even if I have done the best planning in the world.

Such planning includes the more rapid development of managers than would take place through trial and error and passage of time methods. This can include periodic appraisals and incentives of management manpower, early identification of successors to management position, a program for introducing outsiders where they are needed, and the fitting of manpower development needs with over-all corporate growth plans. As Mr. Foster put it:

> Long range planning is a necessity if one's competitive position is to be maintained and improved; and it may prove to be a life-saver if economic conditions—over all or within an industry—should take a turn for the worse.

While this logic is unassailable, it's also important to note that long range planning doesn't mean that the company is thereby fitted for a strait jacket. Flexibility and agility are two essential ingredients in providing against the ill winds of chance.

Helping Your Windfall

It's perfectly true that basing your future on luck alone may be costly if luck runs against you, but this doesn't preclude running with your luck when it makes its shining appearance. Having the wit and agility to move quickly and adapt methods to circumstances is a vital part of helping your windfall and capitalizing on "breaks."

> A small floor tiling company struggled along through the war years into the middle forties with barely enough business to keep its head above water. Shortly after the war the housing boom got under way, and the demand for floor tile rose sharply. Keeping its eye on the rising housing curve, the management went in debt up to its ears to build new plant, hire new help, and modernize. Its most optimistic hopes were exceeded, and within five years was operating at a level far exceeding the growth rate of many of its slower competitors.

Of course, the exact opposite can happen as well. One of the classic stories is that told of Montgomery Ward under the management of Sewell Avery. While Sears was building after the war at a phenomenal rate, the redoubtable Mr. Avery was reported to be lecturing his officers and directors on the necessity for maintaining a high liquid position in preparation for the forthcoming depression. When a store burned down, it was not replaced. No new locations were researched, and none opened. As a result it continually lost market position until after Mr. Avery's retirement and a new management who saw the growth pattern of the economy more lucidly took over.

The real trick is to adapt the manner in which management functions to the circumstances. This is as true in large companies as in small firms, and in individual departments as well as whole corporations.

> Cost reduction seemed to be the major problem in one small company. A consultant studied the situation and discovered that the supervision in the plant was wishy-washy about demanding a fair day's work from the workers. Investigation proved that in the past there had been extensive labor trouble, and the supervisory group had been trained and instructed in a particularly soft approach to human relations, which came out looking like pussy-footing. Presented with these facts, the management instituted a program of improving discipline and rigor. Without returning to the old days which had caused the labor trouble, they began to insist that employees produce according to standards, and that wasteful practices be eliminated. The results were immediate and startling. Among those most pleased were the old time employees who had been dismayed at the new laxity which had followed the human relations binge.

The current debate which rages in management over best methods of supervision, "the hard versus the soft line" in management, seems to be moving in the direction of firmness and discipline. This, in all truth, is probably more a product of the times and of necessity than of any newly discovered principle of management. In management practice there is a time for diplomacy, for cunning, for sincerity, for immediate obedience, for participation. None are universal tools, for all of them must be available to exploit the competitive demands of the circumstance.

> Take the example of the man who entered the construction business through a franchise to sell metal buildings. Seeing further opportunities for profit in laying concrete floors for such buildings he added a floor division. His customers proved interested in other types of buildings as well as the type he sold, so he rushed into the construction business on all types of buildings. All of these things happened to fall into a rising market for contractor work and he was phenomenally successful. Since he had done no investigation into the overall possibilities (he hadn't time) he took a chance of great failure. Yet it paid off handsomely simply because he was impetuous. If he had been prudent, he might still have been a dealer in buildings instead of being a large contractor with substantial assets.

Moral Courage and Luckiness in Leadership

Such instances are often the typical example which is cited to show that a person was lucky in management. Yet, the example of the contractor isn't without a valid principle. It's the axiom that *planning may prevent the ravages of ill luck, but boldness, audacity, energy and a certain amount of fierce drive are needed to exploit good luck.*

Once all the odds have been weighed, the economic and social trends assessed, and the possibilities of gain and loss assessed, *boldness is better than caution.*

P. J. Lovewell, director of economic research at Stanford Research Institute, has this to say about management leadership and courage:

> Occasionally we see a company with all of these visible success characteristics—but it still isn't going anywhere. Plans are carefully prepared by a competent staff; product possibilities of real potential are staked out; the company's record of service is outstanding; and yet progress is disappointing. When this occurs the usual missing ingredients are management leadership and moral courage. In the final analysis planning cannot be meaningful without management foresight, management support, management decision, and management follow-through.

This drive and willingness to assume risks—uninsurable risks—are the basic elements in the management job for which he is paid. Despite the rationalization of management, the division of the management job into logical portions, with staff and line experts in charge of each, there is no escaping the uninsurable risks of being a business man—an *entrepreneur.*

Because large corporations are collective in their efforts they are prone to the conservator's viewpoint. Cooperation between many people to make the organization operate at all makes the center of power and decision more difficult to identify. Many of the risks they take are less serious in the overall life of the organization since they have resources to ensure its success through simple ponderousness and persistence in overcoming obstacles. The ever pressing need in such an organization is a corps of men scattered throughout its ranks who are impelled by the instincts of the business entrepreneur. These are the traders, the risk takers, the profit seekers who will exercise their talents as employed managers with the same zeal and boldness which they would exercise if the gains were to be their own.

The quality which seems to be most associated with the lucky executive is not one of forbearance and restraint. It is performance and action.

18

How to Keep and Use a Secret

"Trust not him with your secrets, who when left alone in your room turns over your private papers."
—JOHN LAVATER

One of the troublesome problems for the executive in the modern corporate business system is handling information with discretion and judging what should or should not be considered secret. This is no simple dilemma, for the modern executive who wants to rise through the great organization, at the same time he hopes to make his personal imprint upon it, is faced with a paradox with regard to *information*. On one hand he knows that the organization runs on participation and committees to a large degree. On the other if he tells everything he knows he limits his progress to that which any good conformist can make if his radar is tuned to the proper signals from the mass of people in management.

The hard fact is that conspicuous and personal leadership that makes things happen through organization requires that the man who would develop his skill at rising and achieving must not only confide, he must "communicate." From another viewpoint, for the executive to build and extend his orbit of control he must at times withhold information and facts which might transfer control from himself to the group. This control from a man to a committee or a team all too often has the effect of deadening the impact of leadership and vitality in the firm, substituting in its place a sort of administrative nudist camp where such old fashioned virtues as privacy, secrecy, and circumspection may be considered as an evidence of maverick behavior, and a violation of many companies' concept of the accepted pattern of leadership.

Consider the plight, for example, of the man who would make things happen who must function in a firm where, as one president put it:

"Our company is managed by communication. We do not have leaders over people, but working with them."

Naturally the manager who would make things happen must pay some token obeisance to such statements. At the same time he mustn't take it too seriously to the point where he allows the norms of the organization to be his own, or he will discover that he does indeed merely work with people rather than moving them. The climate of course must be one of candor and thoughtful answers to questions which the employee requires in order to perform his duties and understand reasons for policy. Yet, the leader must ever retain the seventh veil beyond which he withdraws occasionally to formulate goals toward which he will persuade, direct, order, cajole, or manipulate people. This places him under some tension in deciding what matters are secret and which are not.

Handling the Enjoined Secret

Perhaps the first level of problems in managing secrets is the matter of the enjoined secret, in which the manager is privy to information with the direct understanding that it will not be divulged by him. A new product has been developed in research and will be marketed in six months. He is invited to a briefing session—sworn to secrecy—and allowed into the temple. Obviously this is one which he may use only through taking preparatory steps for the forthcoming changes which will result from the new product without telling anyone below him the reasons for the steps. Perhaps he cuts back on improvement project budgets for existing products which will soon become obsolete. Despite the puzzlement of engineers who would prefer to continue their project to completion he must cover his reasoning with an appearance of confusion, incompetence, or outright lies.

Perhaps one ancillary rule here is that there are certain kinds of information which a manager should be cautious about in letting himself be sworn to secrecy upon. Matters such as confronted one bank personnel officer might illustrate this.

> Mr. Jones, personnel manager in a large firm, was asked for an appointment by the lady who was president of the employee credit union. Upon entering his office she said:
> "I've got to ask that you promise not to repeat what I'm going to say to you."
> Foolishly the personnel man promised, perhaps thrilled by the confidence being placed in him by this old and loyal employee.
> "I've been stealing from the credit union's accounts," she stated, "and am $450 out of pocket. I'm so glad that *you* know it, too."

Respecting confidences is a virtue under some circumstances, but it requires that the manager have in mind the possibilities for the future if he accepts or seeks out secret information accompanied by any such promise of secrecy extracted in advance. Matters which make him an accomplice, whether to a crime or simply to something inimical to the company or himself, are to be avoided like the plague, and once received should not be accepted quietly and tucked away in the inner compartment of the mind without further action.

Loyalty to persons is an admirable trait. Yet, this same loyalty extended to "the organization" often results in immense stress upon the manager. This is more than simply refraining from shipment of defective products to customers, which most companies do not desire to do. Nor does it merely limit itself to avoidance of unethical practice or sharpness in commerce which the typical corporation today does not approve. It does extend to having a sense of responsibility to individual dignity of people which occasionally runs into conflict with the organization.

> Take the instance of old Gary X who was performing poorly, and was being considered for separation. It was decided by the personnel committee that he would be asked to leave after six more months when a suitable replacement would be ready. All members of the committee were sworn to secrecy. Shortly after this his manager, a member of the committee, overheard that Gary had been offered a safe and better paying position with another firm where he might finish his career with dignity. A quick survey of the committee found them adamant against taking any action which might expedite Gary's expulsion in order that he might capitalize upon the offered position. His manager weighed his regard for the man against the integrity of the committee and let Gary pass up the offer.

Others would have handled it exactly the opposite and violated the committee rule and tipped off old Gary.

Being Judicious With Information

Practically everyone expresses admiration for the stuff called "communication." This isn't idle talk, for it's part of a larger plan by which most modern corporations run, that the leader gets results through raising the dignity of the individual, giving him information and participation in the affairs which affect him.

Yet the judicious handling of even routine and factual information about the job isn't without its limitations.

> Take the case of the electronics company where the product was a stabilizing device for aircraft used by the navy. The girls working

on the assembly of this equipment were prone to talk incessantly on the job. This worried the management no little bit since a failure of the equipment might cause a plane to go down and even result in a flyer's death.

Determined to communicate the importance of quality they called a meeting, and had a navy officer tell them that if they "didn't stop their talking on the job, they might make a mistake which would cause a naval officer to be killed."

This had the desired effect of stopping the talking, but it was also noted that many of the girls quit their jobs within the next week or two. Upon exit interviews they stated:

"For the money I'm getting I don't want to do work that can kill a sailor if you just turn your head for a minute."

Management threw up its hands. It laid low on communicating stories about drowned sailors, and set up a tight quality control system to catch any defects which might result from the girls talking on the job.

The point is that simply telling people your reasons or letting them in on your secrets doesn't necessarily mean that they will respond by seeing things the same way management does.

Telling people certain types of things can have no effects but harmful ones, and may include such matters as these:

1. Tentative plans which may never be carried out.
2. Information which would help one person against another without benefiting the company.
3. Matters of personal information about employees which come into the hands of management in the course of routine personnel administration.
4. Rumors.
5. Gossip.
6. "Hard facts about the business" which aren't commonly known and which might serve as useful strategic information in the hands of a competitor (technical information, cost data, etc.).
7. Allegations about people or groups which have no solid basis in fact, or remain unproven.

Another pertinent kind of secret for the manager which he might find it wise to be judicious with, is personal information and opinions which, if divulged, would constitute an invasion of his privacy. In the large corporation today there is an almost insatiable desire in the part of many, especially personnel people and psychologists, to probe deeply into the attitudes, motivations, personality traits, and feelings of employees, especially at the managerial level.

Ostensibly this probing is for purposes of predicting success. The pattern goes something like this. The psychologist, trained or otherwise, assumes that certain personality traits will lead to success and others will bring about failure. (In some instances he is right, in others he has no empirical evidence to support his thesis.) He therefore probes into the personalities of men in the organization in order to inventory these attitudes and traits. With this inventory he then recommends promotion, job assignment, or the withholding of such benefits. Privacy becomes nearly impossible for an individual under such circumstances, and constitutes a problem of maintaining secrecy for the individual being put under the microscope.

William H. Whyte once published an article in *Fortune* on "How to Cheat on Personality Tests." It was exactly this protection of personal privacy, call it secrecy if you will, which he pointed up.

> "The important thing to recognize," Whyte points out, "is that you don't win a good score, you avoid a bad one."

Recognizing that the probers are being impertinent in asking you to incriminate yourself and your career chances in the first place, it shouldn't be at all a matter of conscience to judiciously withhold information which will prevent you from getting the job you might like *as long as you are confident that you can handle bigger responsibility*. Here is the real test of how completely you let yourself be exposed by the manipulative devices of the company.

The manager who knows he can make things happen and do a job for the company has a responsibility to be discreet about divulging information about his feelings and habits which might bar him from getting such a position.

Whyte lists six statements which might, if kept firmly in mind, get you through the majority of such tests and interviews.

a. I loved my father and mother but my father a little more.
b. I like things pretty well the way they are.
c. I never worry much about anything.
d. I don't care for books or music much.
e. I love my wife and children.
f. I don't let them get in the way of company work.

Since most psychologists, selecting people for organization man jobs, won't understand in the slightest the leader who has unique personal confidence enabling him to make things happen despite the strictures of conformity and committee forms of management, it's pointless to play into his hands.

Perhaps the kind of secret which is most vital to keep in personal advancement strategy is the kind that responds to such questions as "What are your major weaknesses?" Don't for heaven's sake give any real ones, such as the fact that you are afraid of the dark. It's far safer to invent a few which seem to be assets to the investigator, but which you list as liabilities. "Sometimes I am too energetic in getting my work done." Don't overdo this to the extent that you let slip your opinion, "When I get in charge here I'll knock a few heads together and clean out the gold bricks." This is entirely too much dominance, and will indicate to the interviewer an unhealthy desire for control.

When to Give in Order to Get

Being in the mainstream of useful information in an organization means you are able to tap and use the information flowing along the grapevine. This means two things.

1. You must know where the grapevine is and how it operates.

2. You must not appear to be an originator, not even a vital link in the process. Yet you must be able to offer a morsel occasionally in order to get some in return.

The problem here lies in the possibility that you may inadvertently find that you are really letting slip more than you are getting, thereby becoming a generator of major importance. Usually there are two or three places which you can tap to get most of the useful information on what's going on that will give you some tactical advantage. Such crude tactics as picking over wastebaskets and thumbing through papers on another's desk are gauche, and inevitably result in a closing of the channels. An occasional crisis may arise where the ability to read material upside down is of some value, but even these are to be considered as unlikely sources of information of great worth.

Probably the best source of information is from the horse's mouth itself. Most executives and staff people have trouble guarding their remarks to the degree that they can't be patched up into a consistent story that's useful to know. Naturally this requires some extensive personal contact with the man, and the luncheon table and golf course are places where you will be tapped without your knowing it, and in return you can construct a picture from the parts. Coffee breaks are often occasions for the rumor mill to grind. Under such circumstances it's wise to be able to give something in order to get more.

From our knowledge of how the grapevine works, it functions through "clusters" of people, reports Dr. Keith Davis. One person tells three or four others. Only one of the cluster will repeat the rumor and pass it along, the remaining members of the cluster will keep it to themselves. Such carriers of rumor and secrets operate through the firm so that the grapevine is probably only made up of one-fourth or so of the employees. Yet it carries the tales it bears to the entire group through the cluster phenomena.

This particular individual in the cluster, sometimes identified by the social scientists and the "liaison individual" is more apt to dispense gossip, rumor, and secret information than others. Other people in the work group seem to have a lot of influence over the opinion of others beyond this, and are resource persons when it comes to interpretation and conjectural materials on what's apt to happen around the office.

This leads to a principle in getting and using secret information:

If you are going to be ahead of the crowd in getting inside information, you must be a liaison person with the grapevine.

Now this may provide you with inside information and afford you the opportunity to get something through giving something else by way of information. It also is a distressing fact that such people who function as transmitters through their cluster can't remain anonymous to others for long. You become known as a "link" and accordingly over time this means you will be labelled as a person from whom the really vital information is withheld.

In short, in order to get and use secrets you will need to become a rather specialized form of carrier of information. This means that you'll want to be known only to a select few and with them for only useful stuff. The important thing to remember here is that you shouldn't use the grapevine as an ordinary person might—to fill a psychological need for knowing the gossip or relieving some emotional strain within you. For the manager who sees the secret and the inside information as a tool of action and control, it's a form of intelligence activity which he manages quietly but in an orderly fashion.

Since the rumor mills are ordinarily quite thorough, even for the receiving members of the cluster, there's no necessity for joining the carrier chain in order to be kept abreast of what the grapevine is saying. The only requirement is that you belong to a cluster which is serviced by an efficient carrier. In this capacity you can get all of the important material without giving anything in return. You won't get it first (that requires that you be a carrier) but you'll get it quite soon. Only the "loner" who has no cluster never hears what's running along the informal channels, and through the rumor mill.

The Hardest Secret to Keep

The rumor which comes to a manager can often be handled without comment or simply by saying, "Hm, isn't that interesting?" It's not as easy to keep a particular kind of secret in which everyone knows that you have information or could make a decision which must ultimately be announced, but for purposes of timing mustn't tell just now.

Surprisingly the hardest secret to keep isn't the one which is not even known to exist, but the secret which everyone suspects exists and upon which they feel enough confidence to make a direct question asking for facts. The reverse of this is true also:

The best way of finding out a secret is to ask a man who knows one.

Turning down information is a tough job for anyone. Unless he has been especially reinforced in his determination to keep the matter absolutely silent he is very apt to tell it to a person who asks him point blank for the facts. Occasionally he may add lamely, "Now this isn't known yet, and I must ask you to keep it quiet, but . . ." At this point the secret probably isn't a secret anymore, but you've cracked the silence barrier and can put the information received into use in your personal planning. It's a hard-shelled or especially enjoined person indeed, who can resist communicating what he knows in today's company. Certainly it's more honest, clean cut and simpler if you want to know a secret to go right to the person who knows and ask him. Surprisingly often things that are presumed secret will prove to be somewhat less restricted than you supposed.

The other side of this coin is that others will have discovered this fact if they've thought about it at all. In this case, keeping a secret may require that you plan in advance how to resist such raids on your storehouse of secret information. In some instances you're just as apt as the next fellow to let slip information with the provision that the hearer not repeat it. It's a wise idea to have your response planned. Simply saying, "I can't say," or some similar response will do if you are armed for inquiries and are determined not to lie nor divulge your information.

There are several categories of what might be termed hard-to-keep secrets.

1. *The I-told-you-so type.* A manager of marketing argues against a certain line of promotion and predicts that it will rebound to the com-

pany's disadvantage if tried. Sure enough it fails and the bad results are barely in before he's telling people I-told-you-so. Along with this crowing, he's also letting slip some other information about sales, profits, or other techniques which he should keep his lip buttoned about.

2. *The hurray-for-me type.* This secret is hard to keep because telling it provides a boost to the ego of the teller. He has scored a victory or a coup over his opponents and wants to let others know what a great man he is. Perhaps its a promotion that's all fixed but hasn't been announced yet. This is often prefaced by, "It hasn't been officially announced yet but . . . "

3. *The bad-news-for-you type.* In one eastern plant the executive committee decided to let a vice president go. Since he was out of town it was decided that it should be kept secret until he was told. When the president finally called him into his office and informed him the next morning, the ex-V. P. reported sourly, "Yeah, I heard it from the elevator man on my way in this morning."

Small Talk

Perhaps the most fertile source of rumors and information which ought to be kept secret is the small talk which comprises the lubricant for human relations on the job. Small talk which turns to the company often finds itself turning to matters of speculation and personalities. Often the small talk circuit and pattern can develop independently of any information or factual support the best-kept secret. Let's take the case of the large chemical company where three executives were competing for the general manager's position. During the six weeks ahead of the final decision for this position one of the competitors carried off an especially clever coup over several competitors. He not only stole several valuable customers thereby, but he pulled the organization along with him to make the new deliveries on time. As a result everyone speculated that he was now the number one competitor for the promotion.

When, in fact, he received the promotion, which had been a carefully guarded secret insofar as the top management was concerned, it came as a surprise to no-one. Here was a case where everyone was able to anticipate what the answer would be as accurately as the top group, and any attempt to keep it a secret would have been foolish. Stock splits when a stock runs over 100, are often predictable from experience of past actions of the same kind, and are difficult to keep under cover simply because small talk both inside and outside the company concludes—independently—that it will happen.

Social scientists have often been amazed at the accuracy of conclusions reached by the small talk circuit, which exists quite independently of the grapevine in that it needs no feeders, clusters, or transmitters to have everyone arrive at the same independent result. A fight between executives, even when conducted in secrecy is often the topic of small talk and independent observations that senses the state of affairs without any outside feeder adding to the input of facts.

If the secret then is one that is being commonly chatted about in small talk through independent speculation, it's not really a secret and should be verified or denied wherever possible.

This is most often true of "talk" involving the reputation of key people in the organization in their personal lives. Take the case of the executive who was reputed by the small talk circuit to be an alcoholic. No single "bit" of information toured the grapevine to verify this opinion. He was seen once by the secretaries reeling into a restaurant where they had gone for a hen-party dinner. Several people had run into him in the men's lounge drinking Alka-Seltzer early in the morning. Some visitors noticed liquor on his breath another morning shortly after starting time. Without any organized story running the grapevine the accumulated small talk concluded that he had a serious drinking problem.

Small talk has the characteristic of being different from the grapevine in that it wells up independently in numerous places at once without any single bit of information being transferred from ear to ear by a hidden communication chain. It reflects the sense of the group that something is so, and often the best guarded secret, well preserved from any leak to the grapevine, may be commonly known through this welling up in the small talk which goes on constantly in the organization. Keeping the obvious, and sometimes the subtle, from getting through the grapevine still may not quiet its being known and accepted throughout the ranks if small evidences of the truth are available to casual, but sensitive, observers.

Secrets Versus Good Communication

In the light of these complex methods by which information is transmitted despite the best efforts of a few individuals to keep it from being known, the question then arises as to the balance which must be maintained for effective operations. Secret information which is impossible to maintain as confidential requires useless and pointless energy and effort on the part of many people. Where information is apt to be leaked or presumed true with some accuracy, it's often the best plan to deal with it frontally and let everyone in on the facts. Take the case of communicating with management people during labor negotiations. Closed meetings are held, offers made, and counter-proposals given in return. Some companies now make it a point to issue bulletins and statements to foremen during the progress of negotiations. As a director of industrial relations for one firm puts it:

> They'll find out anyway from the workers who learn it from the union. We might as well tell them the straight facts rather than keep them in suspense, and letting them feel that they are less well informed than employees on the bench.

News of impending changes have greater impact to the employee if he gets the facts immediately after the decision is made from the company than if he hears it indirectly from another worker.

Despite the necessity of maintaining silence on certain kinds of information, the situation in most firms is that more information should be transmitted openly and quickly.

Integrity and Secrecy in Leadership

The guides to the maintenance of secrecy in leadership bring us into confrontation with the issue of integrity and what constitutes intellectual and personal morality in such matters on the part of the leader who makes things happen. Henry Taylor, the English statesman, suggests that there are two classifications of conscience; a strong conscience and a tender conscience. The man with the overly tender conscience may be illustrated in management by the manager who pays too much attention to the small responsibilities at the expense of his larger responsibilities.

> Take, for example, the man whose conscience winces at asking people what in his heart he knows he would detest doing himself, such as dealing with unpleasant customers, discharging old time employees or closing a plant in a small town which is the major source of employment.

Because he winces at this, he usurps most of the dirty jobs himself, or even fails to step up to his larger responsibility of preserving the health and vitality of the firm in the competitive market. He lacks the capacity to be cruel in order to be kind, and in this ends up in being ultimately the cruelest of all leaders.

Often this conscience, which is all tenderness and has no strength, will breed in its holder a great tendency toward inaction and become a "quagmire in which the faculty of action shall stick fast at every step."

Under such a man secrecy often becomes a guide for inaction and the man who wouldn't hurt a fly will hurt the whole company and the economy. Because he anticipates the response of people so accurately he flinches from saying what needs saying and spreads a tender cloak of anonymity over what should be said forthrightly. Secrets which protect others overly much or create a false sense of security among those concerned is a perfectly wrong result which comes from an overly tender conscience.

Here too lies many of the areas of misunderstanding between the social scientist and the business leader. The social scientists have, by and large, a tender conscience. The business leader who makes things happen must have a strong conscience. The blows and cuts which are suffered by individuals in the modern company in terms of its ego and social needs, are often the only concern of the social scientists who enter the business firm to study what goes on there. He is almost wholly insensitive (especially when he's there to inculcate managers in sensitivity) to the rationale and virtues of the strong conscience. This leads to different perception about the extent to which managers must communicate, both in urging too much, and in urging too little as the conscience of the observer permits.

The action-oriented manager deals with the problems of secrecy, in short, through developing a sense of integrity which is controlled by a strong conscience rather than a tender one.

19

How to Pick a Fight
and Win in Business

"With the jaw of an ass have I slain a thousand men."
—Judges XV:16

Practically nobody talks about the subject of fighting in business. It's normally considered naughty, and furthermore it is implied, shouldn't be done at all. This folklore, that fighting leads to career oblivion, is in diametric opposition to the basic fact of business in a free society. Competition is in fact nothing more than defeating another through economic superiority, greater agility, being quicker witted, a sharper tongue, or having more resources than the other fellow. Conflict of wills is—however much we may disguise it—a basic act of business management with the minor exceptions of certain complete monopolies. It's further a product of the immense upward striving of many people for the lucrative and high status positions in the hierachies of business. The prizes for top leadership positions are great. It's not surprising then that competition and rivalry for them should be quite fierce.

Despite the underlying facts about fighting—call it by any name—there are certain rules of the game which the others in the forest expect will be followed. Since they have the capacity to throw their weight in favor of one protagonist or another, and all the scrapping is done in close quarters where others can alter the outcome, it's part of the strategy of competition not to violate the rules of the fray. Learning such rules early is part of the personal development of the manager who would make things happen. Let's look at a few of the unwritten rules which govern the rules of economic warfare for managers.

Rule One: Always express abhorrence of fighting. Perhaps the cardinal guide to successful combat in business is the avoidance of any outward appearance of relishing combat. It's more a matter of outward mien than inward emotion, in fact it is a unique combination of pugnacity and driving ferociousness inwardly masked by an outward cloak of complete affability and congeniality. The more completely this split in inward attitude and outward manner can be managed, the more acceptable it will be to those who surround you.

Rule Two: Avoid petulance and impatience. In entering the frantic world of business competition, it's wise to take special pains to master one's emotions in order that no glimmer of petulance, impatience or sullenness appear, no matter how severe the blow received. For a manager to sulk over getting beat out of a promotion, losing an account, or being transferred to the Unimak, Alaska sales office will immediately arouse murmurs of clucking regret from his peers. "Maturity" in business competition means a self control over disappointment or chagrin which goes far beyond the phlegmatic and stolid control of the German saber duelist when he receives a fierce hack from his opponent. In business, he must not shout out his dismay and anger, but must behave just as if the outcome were a source of the greatest possible delight. A smile, and hearty handclasp, with eye contact are part of the ritual. Later, over a couple of highballs with his wife, he may express his true sentiments, but with everyone from around the shop it's *de rigeur* to accept such blows with aplomb.

Rule Three: Never lose your temper. Fighting in business is disguised in affability and losing one's temper is prohibited. This means more than simply refraining from saying nasty things. Anger is easily detected, since it entails a whole sequence of physiological changes in the person. The mechanism of the sympathetic nervous system makes chemical and electrical changes in the body when one gets angry. Adrenalin is shot into the blood stream, the liver injects fuel into the system, breathing increases, blood circulation rises, discoloration of the face and enlargement of the veins take place, and the salivary and digestive juices flow haltingly. All of these make changes in the person which can be seen, and indicate that he really can't control himself. In even the most composed person, anger may raise signals such as a reddening of the ears, or a hearty belch for the ulcerous, which are signals to the cool observer that one's hackles have risen under competition. Thus the other person is armed to deal more rationally and compete even better by appealing to those acts which bring on anger. The truly composed and sophisticated fighter in business never lets the message get into his sympathetic nervous system. He remains rational, calm, and affable.

Rule Four: Winning is what counts in the long run. Among the small group of people who know the rules, winning may be interpreted to cover a lot of actions, only a few of which have to do with genuine regard for others. Over the lóng haul it's winning which seems to be the most acceptable, and doing so with composure. The kinds of infighting and hanky-panky which schoolboy ethics or ordinary love of one's fellow man dictate, can be reconstructed later through good behavior once one is securely on top. There are some rules for *winning* in business too:

1. *Keep your value systems in line.* However much lip service you may pay to serving others, the successful fighter for status and position must remember the priority system which ranks:

   himself first
   the company next
   any other casual human who happens to be present, third.

2. *Hard work is a great competitive weapon.* In winning promotions and rank, being a veritable beaver, a secret weapon, sometimes downgraded by cynics, is of highest importance. The brief case carried home and work done by midnight oil arms its bearer with facts, insights, and know-how which comprises an armor which will stand him in good stead.

3. *Keep your eye on the main chance.* The executive who would rise must always keep his eye squarely on the road ahead and seek out opportunities for scoring hits. The "main chance" seeker is a man who wants to get rich or important himself, and is willing to make money for the company as a means of getting his own reward. (The social scientists call this "reconciling the goals of the individual with that of the organization.")

4. *Build strong alliances.* Despite the competition between executives, there are certain kinds of alliances on non-competitive matters which must be made and maintained. Exchanging information on management methods, as is done at American Management Association meetings, or joining the Toastmaster's Club improves oneself at the same time it improves others. These alliances are vital in building a reputation among others since they provide a forum for proving one's mastery of business methods.

5. *Look good in performance—not on appearances alone.* There are

many who contend that it's fatal to look *too good,* be too well dressed, be too handsome or be too glib in speeches. The "model manager" on his way up attracts the javelins of the lesser lights— many of whom will never make it. Nevertheless, they constitute— like a stream filled with flesh-eating piranhas—a total influence which should never be aroused through attracting too much attention through making big splashes. In one firm one such superior-appearing man constantly attracted attention of the type that caused people to ask, "How can anybody be that good? Let's look for some flaws in his facade." Naturally they found some, and he was routed into a safe niche where he worked for his competitors who hadn't made the mistake of looking too close to perfection.

6. *Look conformist—think maverick.* Attracting attention through odd appearance, non-conformist behavior, and erratic actions is to invite being slapped down. At the same time, in order to win, the up and coming executive must constantly generate new and successful ideas, which means that he doesn't let group thinking dominate his own instincts.

7. *Don't relax when winning.* Once your strategy has begun to pay off, and you are gaining the recognition and prizes, don't sit back and enjoy them. Pour your new resources into making further advances, building up a team to run with you, and making breakthroughs into new territory.

Rule Five: Fight to win, not to kill. The rule of affability can be extended to include behavior toward the loser as well as the victor. Reactions always occur when the winner wastes his effort and energy in getting revenge upon those who competed hard but lost. The trick after victory is to convince the losers that they lost to a better man, and win them over as allies. This becomes apparent as the winner notes the value system outlined above. The first priority is getting on top oneself, and the second is to advance the interests of the firm. Destroying capable men simply because they fought and lost can result in many good men being thrown out and into the hands of a competing company. To execute such a policy overtime would only serve to weaken the company and ultimately react to the disadvantage of the executive himself. Since he must get results through others' efforts he must be careful not to destroy everyone he passes by in his rise to the top, lest he weaken the organization that must be his to run after he has succeeded.

Rule Six: Gather allies by perpetuating the rules for competition. The rules of competition and fighting in business are of course designed to assist the superior man in rising, and in maintaining his status in the organization. It's therefore distinctly to his advantage to support vigorously the unwritten code of fighting. In doing so he insures that he will rule over a stable and successful organization in which able men will rise, and the less able will level off according to their abilities.

Rule Seven: Always consolidate your captured ground. The fight to move in the organization is almost always disruptive and may result in uneasiness and grumpiness among those not chosen. It's imperative then that the top man, immediately upon assuming that post, sort out such problems and solve them.

> Take the case of the vice president who was selected as president of a small company after a period of several months of doubt as to which of several vice presidents would be chosen. Even before the retirement of the outgoing president, the president-elect began a campaign of punishing the failing candidates. As a result two of them quit and many other people in the organization stated that they had a great feeling of insecurity about the future.

Consolidating captured ground in business competition between individuals, unlike that between companies, may require that changes be introduced cautiously.

Conflict of wills, conflict of interests, and of personalities are a normal condition of the world of business. Learning the arts and the skills of successfully meeting such situations, and teaching them to the up and coming, is part of the way in which a successful executive makes things happen in business.

20

How to Make a Decision

"There are divers kinds of decisiveness; there is that of temperament, and that of reason, and there is that which is compounded of both, and this last is best..."

—HENRY TAYLOR (1836)

Recent literature on decision-making in management has laid great stress upon the rational aspects of decision making. "Get the facts, weigh and decide, take action, and follow through," so went the famous course which was offered foremen by the hundreds of thousands during World War II. New decision-making courses, taught by playing management games in which answers are produced from the bowels of a computer, or simply mathematical exercises to substitute "minimax" for intuition in decisions, are part of this new apparatus of decision making.

None of these approaches, however laudable they may be from the viewpoint of improving rationality, attack the central block to decision making which makes, or fails to make, things happen in an administrative situation. For the executive who gets things done, there are habits and patterns of behavior that make the proper mix of fact gathering and decision in which his reflexes move surely from facts to action without undue haste, not the deliberation and delay which marks the indecisive person.

For most managers this cycle of decision making to get things done is a *compressed* running of the cycle of thought and decision which has the appearance of elimination of certain key steps. Yet the manager who makes things happen makes more right decisions than wrong ones. It's this ability to compress time in adhering to the safest procedures for decision making that mark the action-getting executive. What, then, is in this decision making process that makes for both fast and good decisions?

This should be followed by the logical question, once you know the process how can you compress the time for decisions in order that each turn of events may be capitalized upon?

First, the cycle of decision making:

- orientation to the situation
- identification of the key facts
- identification of the major problem or problems
- proposal of possible causes and identification of one
- the scanning of probable solutions
- the aggressive application of the solution
- checking whether it's right or wrong, and trying again.

Let's look at each of these steps, find any pitfalls in them, and take some examples from actual cases in which executives made good decisions that paid off for their organization.

Decisions on Familiar Ground

The experience of most managers is that they can make better decisions on familiar ground than on strange subjects, or in strange environments. The sales manager of thirty years experience, consciously or not, is basing his decisions upon his complete familiarity with the situation in which he operates. He knows perfectly well without consciously setting them out all of the possible causes of the problem, and some of the pitfalls which befall the unwary. In a single instant his mind feeds up into its consciousness a vast potpourri of experiences and strong impressions made to him over the years. Such decisions made on familiar ground are said to be rooted in the experience of the decision maker, and often account for the speed, accuracy, and brilliance of the decision. How then can a satisfactory decision be made when one is confronted with a new situation?

When making decisions on unfamiliar ground, it's necessary to give oneself a complete orientation to the situation.

In other words, the substitute for long experience is an ability to master the facts and attitudes involved in as short a time as possible. With such orientation to the situation two things emerge for the less experienced person.

- His intuition and intelligence in problem solving give him some inkling into the probably satisfactory results or conditions in the situation.

- He identifies the key facts which indicate what conditions should exist if the situation were ideal.

- From this orientation to the situation—perhaps from his experience in similar situations—he begins to see several major gaps between what's right and what exists. These comprise the major problems which must be solved.

Take the case of the company which found itself with overloaded warehouses of product, yet orders were not being delivered because the right products were not on hand. A consultant brought into the situation quickly outlined the major facts as stated briefly above. He saw the problem as being one in which too many of the unnecessary items were being produced, while needed products were being shunted aside. He saw a variety of plausible causes for the trouble, and investigated each one carefully. Finally he concluded that it lay in lack of feedback from the production department to the scheduling section. Orders to run a certain quantity were not being followed, and since the schedule department received no reports of actual performance against schedules, it had no controls which would have prevented over-runs on certain orders at the expense of others.

The procedure here was one which might have been followed by an experienced hand who took the time to organize his approach to become completely familiar with the situation, identify the gap between actual and ideal, and direct action toward closing this gap. In this instance the consultant set up a system of feeding back actual results of production against scheduled amounts to the scheduling department. With a few stiff warnings when over-runs or under-runs occurred, issued to the manufacturing supervisors, the situation straightened itself out.

Everyone had a small piece of the situation, and it was only when the consultant entered the scene and familiarized himself with the entire picture that all of the facts were available in one place which could result in a decision that solved the difficulty.

Making the Momentous Decisions

Such a situation as the production control problem which the consultant faced, however complex it may have seemed, was nevertheless less difficult than many in which managers must take part. Many important decisions are of a type which have no single best solution, and in which facts alone are insufficient basis upon which to choose oue course of action.

Many of the big decisions cannot be made on the basis of fact or experience.

This is because decision making is something apart from problem solving. The kinds of decisions which are made on familiar ground are really tests of problem solving ability, rather than ability to make a decision on a course of action among several alternatives. In some instances these decisions made on familiar ground are made under conditions where it is almost certain that the decision will produce a desired result—or at least a predictable one. In others there is risk of failure or loss which accompanies the decisions. This risk, however, is minimized when the ground is more familiar, since many of the obvious risks have been allowed for and their possible effects circumvented.

Most big business decisions which cause the executive to pause in his decision making process are made under conditions that are neither familiar nor allow for prediction of risk. In fact in many such decisions there is downright *uncertainty* not only about the situation and full facts, but about the possible outcomes of following any specific course of action.

How then, can the executive be one who makes things happen when he faces the possibility of failure, or even possible set-backs to the organization? Under such circumstances there are some basic approaches to decision making which serve to make the big decisions more viable for the action getter.

1. *Assume that what's worked in the past will continue to work.* In the face of uncertainty it's better to assume that the things that have proven successful will continue to be the best—until there is some convincing evidence otherwise. Experimentation with untried methods and unproven men isn't to be done on a wholesale basis in the areas of decision making. If you have a solid man who has performed well in the past, he's apt to be the best bet for carrying the heavy jobs in the future. If one territory has always led the pack in volume and quality you can assume that they'll continue to do so in the future—unless some strong evidence causes you to question that assumption.

2. *Identify the things you know for sure.* Even in every decision in the face of uncertainty there are some hard facts. These can be relied upon and should be identified, labelled clearly, and fixed in mind. They shouldn't be confused with opinions, which are sometimes as firmly held as facts, but are less apt to be reliable.

3. *Pinpoint the areas of decision making which require pure reasoning.* Once the facts are in hand, and opinions labelled as such, the decision in

the face of uncertainty should require clear marking off of the area which can only be concluded from reason, logic, conceptual exercise, discursive logic, and intuition. These should then be defined in as clear and logical language as possible under the circumstances.

4. *Try to find a theory that covers the subject at hand.* Here you are seeking analogies, general precepts which have worked in the past, and generalizations which probably will apply to the decision making situation. Using the right principle, voluntarily, the first time, often pulls into the decision the accumulated experience of the past toward the correct decision in this case.

> In one large meat packing firm the manager of research reported to the board of directors that irradiation of food by radioactive isotopes was making such progress that it warranted a substantial investment in research and development. He further predicted that if the research were successful the entire food business would be revolutionized. The board was faced with the choice of allocating funds to this new idea or to an expanded program of research for conventional research on present methods of preparation and production of meat.
>
> "The principle which I think we must follow," one director said, "is to prepare for changes, without sacrificing the present successful line of business."

Whether or not the board adopted his "principle" isn't relevant. More importantly, they were dealing with an intangible decision in the face of uncertainty, assuming that what worked in the past would continue to work, relying on certain things they knew for sure, and clear identification of the decision as one of "how fast" the innovation of food irradiation would come. The decision in this case was that food irradiation was possible but wasn't imminent within the next couple of years, and therefore the balance should be in favor of present products and a substantial increase in atomic irradiation of meat, but not predominantly so.

5. *Don't underestimate force and action in affecting the decision.* Often the decision is made on the basis of static facts and past experiences, which always works in favor of the conservative decision. This may sometimes overlook the effect of force and action upon the outcome of a decision. The decision that a certain course would be the best one may be a self-fulfilling one if it is turned into aggressive action with vigorous and forceful behavior in attempting to prove that the solution was the best. In the face of uncertainty it may be that any of several decisions will work of the one finally chosen as best, if it is aggressively applied and made to work through force, energy and action by the organization.

In other words, decisiveness itself is an important ingredient in decision making under uncertainty.

The decisions which may be "wrong" often turn out well and a satisfactory result is achieved if they are implemented with force and action. Of course under these circumstances nobody may ever know that the wrong decision was made.

> Take the case of the small ceramic company which was by most standards on the downgrade and ready for the receivers. The board decided to assume that it would succeed if it expanded and went even further into debt for a new kiln. The sales organization was expanded and sharpened up for the expanded capacity. Through hard driving effort and herculean energy they pulled it off, and within two years were well on their way to leading the industry in return on investment. The president reported that numerous bankers and more rational businessmen had advised him to get out with as much as he could recover rather than sink more into the firm. Yet, because they decided to grow rather than fold up, and worked at making it happen, the decision proved to be the correct one. Yet, without the force and action which went into implementing the decision the wrongness of the decision could have proven perfectly accurate.

Don't Look Back

Under such circumstances, it would seem advisable for decision makers under uncertainty, once they have made their decision, not to spend too much time looking back to see if they are too far from shore, or are in danger of being caught. The very act of making a decision work requires a certain blindness to the possibility of failure and the closeness of the wolf to the front door of the executive office. This coolness under fire, willingness to take risks and accept uncertainty without lapsing into indecisiveness, lies behind the success stories of many individuals and firms.

Much of the success of the manager who makes things happen is his obliviousness to the possibility that he has made a wrong turn in the road.

Decision making under conditions of uncertainty in business practically demands that the manager avoid vacillation. Having mapped out his strategy, taken the possible actions of competitors into account, of exerting rationality to its utmost, he then needs to put aside his deliberations and the kinds of reflective, cogitative skills which he applied in the decision making process, and channels his energies into making the decision work. At this point decision making is done for the moment and aggressive leadership to get to the goal is in demand.

This cut-off point in decision making may not be until after some experimenting has been done on a smaller scale to decide whether or not the proposal would work in the larger organization.

> "I always find one department or section where there's a progressive man at the top to try out a new idea," reports one general manager. "If it works there, with good leadership giving it a fair try, I can then put it into action in the rest of the organization."

This testing process which the general manager used offers some other safeguards to the decision making process too. In the hands of a good manager, the idea will have its flaws revealed, and minor alterations can be made. Or it might be that some major loophole which was overlooked in the original planning can indicate a major overhaul of the decision or even scrapping it.

On the other hand once the commitment is made there's little advantage in constantly peering backward and wishing that things had been done differently.

> Take the case of the company which made a wrong decision in its capital budgeting. Admittedly it was working in an area with a few guideposts, but with more uncertainty than certainty. It followed all of the accepted practices of allocating its available capital against the demands upon it, yet found that once it was committed and the money borrowed and spent, it could have done much better. It seems that some new technical developments in their business had been just about on the verge of breaking forth, and they had underestimated this possibility. As a result they were faced with a long haul using equipment which would become more and more uncompetitive. The chairman of the finance committee of the board told the board this:
>
> "It's going to cost us something to get out of this situation, but let's not cry over spilt milk. Let's ask everyone from top to bottom to pull as hard as they know how to get the most out of what we've got, and we'll come out a lot better than if we mope about it."

To waste energy and drive on ruminations about what might have happened if a better decision had been made in the beginning, is as destructive as making the wrong decision in the first place. More people fritter away their time and lapse into indecisiveness playing the mental game of "if only I had done otherwise" rather than make foolish, hasty, or ill-advised decisions.

Rationality alone won't make a decision work, however perfect in its structure and logic. Only leadership and force which result in action will do that.

Why Managers Fear Big Decisions

Putting an end to personal indecisiveness is more a matter of temperament than of rationality. Several distinct causes for this indecisiveness appear to be prevalent among poor decision makers.

- *Lack of a clear cut goal.* Where the manager isn't aware of what the central purpose of the organization is, or what his part in it is supposed to accomplish, he can't act freely. Fear of decision making frequently started with a fear of failure, while at the same time no standards exist to inform him of what failure—or success—consists of.

- *Insecurity in his position.* The manager who doesn't feel that he is held in high regard by his boss, or is uncertain about how long he will hold his position if he makes any form of mistake, will probably be indecisive.

- *The manager is on strange ground.* Often the basis for being afraid to step up boldly to big decisions lies in the strangeness of the environment. The dynamic executive from business who goes to Washington to accept a government job may become timid and wavering in his behavior there, amidst the strange world of politicians and government routines.

- *He doesn't know his authority.* The big decisions often go by the board where the manager isn't aware or wrongly feels that he isn't entitled to make such decisions.

In one company a general manager awaited word from the corporate office on whether he should add to his sales organization. Meanwhile back in the corporate headquarters top management watched his sales figures, anxiously wondering why they weren't rising. When he revealed that he needed more salesmen he was informed: "For heaven's sake go hire them, that's your job."

- *Clinging to the status quo.* People have a tendency to cling tenaciously to what's been done and worked before, and when the decision involves changing the present ways, however slight, there's a fear that the expected benefits may be offset by losses of what's presently in hand.

"My manager of manufacturing obviously isn't doing the job that I want done," said one division general manager. "But I can't just move in and fire him. First I don't know that his understudy is even as good, and to bring in an outsider might be very disruptive and I'd be worse off than I am now."

Often indecisiveness is based upon the fact that things haven't yet come to the state where the man at the top can only tell himself, "I guess I'll do something because I couldn't be any worse off than I am now."

When to Listen to Others

Group-think is a term described by critics of modern group decision making processes to imply that individual decisions are superior to the group decision making processes. This is, of course, a half truth. There will be times when the manager must make his decisions alone. On the other hand there are times when to retire to his cell and reflect and decide alone would be a sheer waste of available talent and experience. What are some guides to the action-oriented manager for determining when to listen to others?

- *Listening is cheap.* The best rule to guide decision making is that listening won't hurt anybody. Even when the aurally received material goes in one ear and out the other, it doesn't harm anything, and helps the person talking. It always opens the possibility that something useful might be said.

- *When listening makes the program stronger.* There are some decisions that will depend upon support and teamwork for the execution. If listening to others' suggestions adds impetus to the execution and gains acceptance for the final decision, it's worth while.

- *When it wins over hostile forces.* One of the best ways of gaining an ally is to ask an enemy for assistance and advice. He'll say things that make him part of the decision as it's finally made and will be identified with it.

- *When the decision to be made is already decided.* During the Korean War one firm had decided to go into defense work up to 20 per cent of its sales volume. Numerous suggestions were made and arguments given for and against going into defense work for several weeks after the decision was made. All were noted and the suggestor thanked seriously.

"It didn't hurt us to listen, and we got a lot of our people involved in what was going to happen. We couldn't make the announcement for several weeks, so being free in listening was a way of keeping everyone happy. Actually they almost all recommended that we do what we were going to do anyhow."

- *When the person talking is an expert.* At many stages in the decision making process careful listening to all ideas and especially from people who know some special facet can improve the decision considerably.

What are some of the kinds of decisions in which listening to a group of others or to single experts is sound strategy? Product research, finance, marketing development, mergers and acquisitions, establishment of personnel policy, purchasing policy, public relations policy, and patent policy are ones in which most managers will want to involve more than their own thinking. The key seems to be that expert advice is desirable.

This kind of listening to others and group decision making is probably less effective when rapid action is needed, when there aren't any experts on the subject matter at hand, or where the results of a bad decision don't seem to be very great. Some examples of these solo decisions might include: buy or not to buy decisions for the purchasing man, to ship or scrap some off-quality work for the vice president of manufacturing, or the granting of a credit rating by the credit manager. There's probably no need to get others' views on a decision where the matter is covered by a policy and seems clear cut in terms of precedents under the policy. The decision has already been made, and it's one of execution, which is more often a matter of individual action.

When to Change a Decision

The decisive manager is probably identified by those who watch him as a man who sticks to a course once he's chosen it. This is a perfectly laudible trait, but it can backfire. Despite the necessity of applying force and action to a decision, there's bound to be an occasion when the use of further force is foolhardy and disastrous. This may be because the decision was wrong in the first place. How can a manager recognize the point when he should back off and change his mind?

First there are some guides on when not to change:

Don't change your mind merely because you're running into obstacles. These can't all be foreseen in detail, and the fact that they're tough ones may not mean your decision or choice of action was wrong. It's just the way the road is strewn.

Don't change your mind under the pressure of such difficulties in execution if it's a problem in execution rather than in the rightness of the goal.

Don't try to redo all of your thinking in a hasty moment, if your decision was made on the basis of carefully developed study and analysis to begin with. You probably won't improve that rationality when you are under stress.

> Take the case of the personnel manager who decided to set up a program of employee meetings to communicate employee benefits to all employees. His surveys showed that the company wasn't receiving credit for all of the fringe benefits it was giving its employees. He decided to arrange a series of meetings, using supervisors as trainers to transmit this information.
>
> As the meetings progressed he discovered that many of the supervisors who were supposed to be doing the communicating weren't doing a good job—in fact were probably doing more harm than good. Rather than scuttling the program, or taking back the job from the supervisor, he quickly prepared a further training session for the supervisors and had them practice and rehearse on each other before trying it on their employees. As a result he had more than the success he imagined possible.

Nevertheless there are times when it becomes obvious that the original decision was wrong, and the decision itself should be changed. What circumstances justify such a switch in plans?

Don't hesitate to change plans if some *important new facts* enter the scene. In one automobile company there were numerous wild-cat strikes in one of the accessory plants. The management decided to meet this problem head on, with firm supervisory actions, discharges where necessary, and a general stiffening of the discipline. The program was under way and meeting some rigid opposition from the union, when suddenly an upheaval in the union officers took place. A new crew moved in and took control. The officers of the new union came to management and asked a letting up of some of the pressure, assuring management that they in turn would put an end to the wild-cats and slow-downs. The company quickly changed its decision to exert pressure upon the employees and as a result a complete turn around in the problem occurred. No more slow-downs or unauthorized strikes occurred.

Don't hesitate to *strike while the iron is hot*. If new opportunities which can extend the benefits of the action appear, it's imperative that the decision and plan be amended to encompass the new opportunity. An aircraft company was in search of a director of research, and, after some mulling over the problem, decided to go outside the firm to hire a top flight man. After numerous contacts with possible candidates they found one from a competitor who declared that not only was he interested but he could also bring seven of his key associates. The decision to hire one outsider was quickly enlarged to include the entire group. As a result their research program was jacked up to a higher level at a single step. The distinct advantage which a manager of action has in decision making over those who view administration in a more passive light is his ability to alter the *cause-effect* nature of decisions. To view this entirely as a linear relationship which always prevails is to ignore the effects of aggressive action, force, and determined behavior on the part of the decision maker to consummate the result of his decision. It would be a major mistake for the manager to allow himself to see decision making as a purely rational process where he has the capacity to make things happen, for this latter quality in itself can make many otherwise quite diffident decisions take on the quality of vitality and life which is needed for their successful execution.

21

See It Big — Keep It Simple

"The first principle of composition, therefore, is to foresee or deter-
mine the shape of what is to come and pursue that shape."

—WILLIAM STRUNK, JR.

Being a man of action is more than a matter of temperament, however important that may be. Many persons of impetuous manner have the qualities which would desire that things happen, and frequently their suggestions are proposed with a view to seeing more happen than presently is being done. Yet this carping at inactivity, railing at inaction and stagnation isn't enough by itself.

Perhaps more importantly the person who would make things happen must have the skills of generalizing from the information he has, and encompassing within his scope of thought more than most people can do under the same circumstances. This frame of mind is one of being able to accurately simplify the general conditions which exist in a social situation, and identifying what is important and what is trivial.

The principal block to this seems to be the vast amount of information which daily assails anyone in the management position. Not only have the skills and tools of the administrator proliferated, but the outside influences which impinge upon the managerial decision increase daily. Among the former are the many new tools and techniques which are being developed and which have been used successfully in many companies. The use of cost accounting, electronic data processing, computers, operations research, systems and procedures, wage and salary administration, motivation research, statistical quality control, organization planning methods, and a myriad of similar complex methods are examples of a small portion of this new technology of management and administration. While they add rationality and system to a world that needs managing, they also bring up the distinct possibility that diversion and side excursion from the principal goal of business may entrap the manager.

In the instance of those outside influences upon businesses and managerial decision-making, the delights of dallying with momentous but peripheral affairs matters from the viewpoint of the firm. Inattention to these outside influences may be fatal it's true, but for the executive whose primary function is to run a business they must almost always be viewed first with a view toward long run growth and survival of his firm. This isn't as narrow as it might seem upon first saying, for such considerations always include those actions on the part of the first which are necessary to the preservation and improvement of the system under which the firm operates.

As a trustee of the firm the executive manages it for others, including stockholders, employees, customers, and the public. This balance between competing demands isn't one of simply balancing them like the famous billiard balls of Alfred Marshall. It means that he must first see the requirements which are made of him by the aggregate of all, and the need for making things happen through his efforts as leader of the firm. Without seeing this basic objective he may become so engrossed or hard pressed in satisfying others that he ultimately dissatisfies all.

The shape of what must be for the executive is simply that the firm must work, must survive, and grow.

Unlike the economic models which classical and theoretical economists would suggest, the firm works, grows, and survives because men make it happen. They make it happen because they have a clear image—clearer than all others—of what can be expected of it, and have a plan for making it occur. This fixity on ends is the only possible rule for remaining free from entanglements in the many details of doing business, making and selling products, dealing with unions and customers, and handling the intricacies of finance. It is furthermore the ultimate test of success or failure of the executive. If he runs a profitable firm, sells good products at a fair price and pays good wages along with the amenities of decent working conditions he has succeeded. If he doesn't do all of these things he will fail no matter which of the other requirements upon him he performs superbly well. Delighted stockholders, employees with high morale, satisfied customers, and a community that is pleased with its corporate citizens are not—any of them—by themselves indicators of managerial success. Keeping this larger objective in mind, and knowing how to make it happen is what makes the good executive.

How to Sift and Screen Information and Opinion

Sub-optimal standards of business performance are being proposed daily for the modern corporation. The firm should take part in civic affairs, it should support colleges and universities, it should employ handicapped and minority groups, it should cut costs and fight inflation, and it should give its employees a chance to participate in the decisions which affect them. No one would dispute the soundness of any of these recommendations under some circumstances.

Nonetheless it's the manager role to remain detached from all of them and assess each against the general standard by which he must be judged. There can be no community donations, or support of colleges, unless the firm is profitable. Participation of employees in the decisions which affect them is excellent to the extent that it doesn't hamper unduly the ability of the firm to produce, work, and do business.

The art of screening the many facts, opinions, and demands upon business then must always be against this general standard for executive results.

When Over-Simplification Becomes Falsehood

The temptations to look for single causes in management are many. Many definitions of management have this defect. "Management means getting results through people," goes one such homily. This reduces the manager as David Moore puts it, to a sort of Tom Sawyer who gets the other kids to paint the fence while he watches. Yet, getting others to work is fruitless unless their efforts are productive and profitable and meet the tests of the entire firm's objectives. The implication here is that the manager's only skill is that of delegation. It leaves unanswered the problem of what the manager does once he's passed out the lesser jobs to others.

"Management means communication," declares another school of thought. While it's perfectly true that managers must have great ability to develop communication channels and methods, this is no test of the success of an executive, since it doesn't exclude the circumstance under which he communicates well but the company fails. Certainly the executive is more than a walking switchboard, or a live servo-mechanism, which turns power off and on. He may actually do this, but his skill at this is not the ultimate test of his right to hold the executive position.

Wrong simplifications on management are over-simplifications, which is a form of deception. Even the title of this book, suggesting that managers make things happen could be construed wrongly if it assumed that in simply making things happen—anything at all—the manager was successfully discharging all that might be demanded of him. The real test comes in assessing whether or not the things which he made happen were the right things, and consistent with the goals of the firm.

Assessing Detail Against the Overview

In action this checking of details, of suggestions, and proposals, the manager may spend much of his time weighing one countervailing demand against another. The sales department wants lower prices and more liberal credit. This must be weighed against the cost figures and manufacturing demands for higher standardization and control, and the need for more profits. The demands for more dividends from stockholders must be weighed against the long run demands for plowed back earnings into research and commercial development. This arbitrator of competing demands in executive rank has more than a position of simple mediator between competing demands. He must weigh all demands against the total demand of the firm for producing goods at a profit, providing jobs, and paying dividends.

In the purest sense he is the paid entrepreneur who allocates scarce resources among many competing demands, and assumes the risk of alternative courses of action. His steps to make things happen are inevitably best when they spur on one part of the organization to bring about a state of balance between them that adds up to more ultimate efficiency for all of them, taken as an integrated unit.

On the Importance of Breadth of Viewpoint

Here lies the key to the so-called executive shortage. Certainly there is no lack of candidates for top management positions. Yet, many aspirants see themselves as generalists when their principal approach is through giving wider scope and enlarging the efficiency of one particular activity of the business. The sales manager who becomes general manager must go through several stages of growth to become successful as the general manager, including an enlargement of perspective which will enable him to trim the sales department's proposals with equal zeal as he would any other department when it is inconsistent with over-all organization goals.

The early identification of people with the potential for generalizing about the functions of the business, and seeing the corporate body as something with a life distinct from its parts, yet inextricably linked to them, is at the heart of the executive shortage. This is the lowest hurdle which the successful general manager must overcome. Beyond this comes the even more sophisticated art of seeing these competing demands and making things happen in the organization despite and because of these special claims upon the executive. Basically these skills of generalization and breadth of viewpoint have six characteristics:

- *They are goal-setting skills.* The executive is able to see the corporate entity and all its parts and sets goals for the total organization which are attainable.

- *They are organization skills.* Seeing the complex structure in its entirety, the successful executive is able to integrate them into a shape which he envisions as being the most effective one, and filling the slots in the whole organization with able people who can perform their function well.

- *They are standard makers.* With his organizational shape fixed and made, and staffed with able men, the executive is able to set and transmit standards of performance for the people in the organization, and set goals which require their best abilities to fulfill.

- *They know how to measure.* In the face of this complex structure and the many different people manning it, he is able to inform the organization and himself how well it is performing. He has controls and measuring methods which indicate when the organization is performing up to standards, and when they are falling short of the organization goals.

- *He is an improver.* The broad-gauged manager is an improver of what exists. Where he has set standards he seeks to bring people up to their maximum capacity in order that they meet these standards and develops their personal abilities in order that they will achieve what they set out to do.

Relating the Organization to Society

Perhaps one of the most difficult generalizing skills of the manager is to know his organization intimately and relate its efforts and goals to the over-all goals of the society in which it functions. Industry does not create wealth. God creates wealth, and industry converts it into useful objects through establishing and managing for the benefit of the society in which it functions. Just as society draws on industry for its standard of living, so does the corporation draw on the society for accumulated capital, stable money, and banking systems, an educated and intelligent work force, law and order, sound legal systems, and property rights to acquire and dispose of its assets as it sees fit.

This larger responsibility becomes almost impossible for any single unit of the firm to accomplish without the stated policies of enlightened and action-oriented management to make it happen.

INDEX

212

T

Taylor, Frederick, 27
Taylor, Gordon R., 68
Taylor, Henry, 187
Taylor, Irwin, 98-99
Teamwork, 91-93
Textile mills, 15
Thornton, Charles, 97
Time magazine, 56
Timing, 137
Tough-mindedness, 52-54
Truman, Harry S., 135

U

Unexpected, planning for, 172-174
Unionization, 30
University of California, 144
University of Michigan, 8, 24n., 50,
    108, 118, 144
  School of Business, 38
University of Minnesota, 67
Updegraff, Robert, 36
Uris, Auren, 102
Urwick, Lyndall, 109
U. S. Congress, 12
U. S. Steel Co., 35, 118, 172

V

Value systems, in American society,
    47-48
Vision, 207-210

W

Wade, Charles, 34
Wakeman, Frederick, 132
Watson, Tom Jr., 6
Wealth, 210
  desire for, 164-166
Weston Instruments, 169
Whyte, William H., 181
Wilson, Charles, 125
Winning, 117
  desire for, 120-121
Withdrawal, 42-43
Woodman, H. B., 97
Worker:
  definition, 61
  productivity of, 14
Work habits:
  changing, 78-83
  improving, 79
  leadership and, 83
Work pattern, 79
Worldliness, management and, 11-12,
    30, 35
World War II, 16, 30, 116, 194
  Job Instruction Training programs,
    94

Y

Yale University, 52, 84, 148